CONTENTS

More Than Conquerors	
A Journey of Faith and Growth	
How to Approach This Devotional	
More Than Conquerors	1
Part 1: Embracing God's Victory	2
Part 2: Living with Purpose and Power	3
Part 3: Becoming More Like Christ	4
Part 4: Walking in the Light of Eternity	5
True Freedom in Christ	6
Breaking the Chains of Fear	10
Trusting God in the Waiting	14
Finding Rest for Your Soul	18
Overcoming Doubt with Faith	22
Finding Joy in the Midst of Trials	26
Surrendering Control to God	30
The Power of Gratitude	34
Walking in Forgiveness	38
Embracing God's Peace in the Storm	42
Living with Purpose	46
Renewing Your Mind	50
Strength in Weakness	54

The Power of Prayer	58
Walking by Faith, Not by Sight	62
Finding Hope in God's Promises	66
Finding Contentment in Every Season	70
Overcoming Fear with Faith	74
The Gift of God's Grace	78
The Joy of Obedience	82
Trusting God's Timing	86
The Peace That Surpasses Understanding	90
Finding Strength in God's Presence	94
The Power of Perseverance	98
The Blessing of Humility	102
Loving Others as Christ Loves Us	106
Resting in God's Promises	110
Finding Joy in God's Presence	114
Renewing Your Hope in Difficult Seasons	118
Living a Life of Purpose	122
Walking in the Light of God's Truth	126
Finding Strength Through Surrender	130
The Power of Speaking Life	134
Standing Firm in Faith	138
The Joy of Serving Others	142
Faith Over Fear	146
The Gift of God's Forgiveness	150
Living in the Power of the Holy Spirit	154
Trusting God in the Unknown	158
Overcoming the Lies of the Enemy	162
The Power of Persistent Prayer	166

Living a Life of Gratitude	170
Becoming a Vessel of God's Peace	174
Strength in Waiting	178
Faith That Moves Mountains	182
Living in God's Strength	186
The Beauty of God's Creation	190
Trusting God's Plan	194
Walking in the Light of God's Word	198
The Power of Unity in Christ	202
The Promise of God's Faithfulness	206
Equipped for the Battle	210
Strength in Fellowship	214
Who You Are in Christ	218
Walking in Obedience	222
The Victory of the Cross	226
Living with Eternal Perspective	230
Free from Condemnation	234
Faithful with What You Have	238
The God Who Never Changes	242
Finding Joy in Hardships	246
The Power of God's Grace	250
Trusting God in Uncertain Times	254
Being a Light in a Divided World	258
Starting Fresh: A Journey with Christ	262
Epilogue: A Life Transformed by God	266
Daily/Weekly Planner Page Layout	269
Reflection & Journaling	270
Hymn: More Than Conquerors	274

MORE THAN CONQUERORS

This is not a book about religion.

It's about *reality*—the reality of the Kingdom of God breaking into a fallen world, and the calling placed on every believer to walk not in fear, but in victory. We are not saved to sit—we are saved to *stand*, to fight, and to conquer.

Jesus never said the end would come when Christianity as a religion spreads to the nations. He said the end will come when **"this Gospel of the Kingdom"** is preached (Matthew 24:14). There's a difference. The Gospel of the Kingdom is not just about forgiveness—it's about transformation. It doesn't stop at salvation—it demands surrender. It isn't about attending church; it's about becoming the Church, clothed in power and authority, walking in obedience to the King.

In an age where many confuse church attendance with discipleship and good morals with righteousness, this book is a call back to the truth. A reminder that we are not weak, passive believers waiting for escape—we are **more than conquerors** (Romans 8:37), called to live with boldness, holiness, and Kingdom purpose.

The religious will always try to measure righteousness with a checklist. But Scripture says plainly: *"By the works of the law no one will be justified."* (Romans 3:20) Just like Jonah and the people of Nineveh, sometimes those who encounter the raw mercy of God—outside the walls of tradition—respond with greater repentance than those who hear sermons every Sunday.

I've held onto this message for a while, knowing it wasn't quite complete. But after speaking with a spiritual mentor of mine—someone whose wisdom and walk with God I deeply trust—I finally believe this devotional is ready. Their confirmation was the last piece I needed to release it in faith.

So this is your invitation. Not to a system. Not to a denomination. But to the Kingdom.

Let's reclaim what it means to follow Christ—not as fans, but as warriors. Because the battle is already won, and it's time we start living like it.

A JOURNEY OF FAITH AND GROWTH

Welcome to this devotional—a 52-chapter journey designed to guide you into a deeper relationship with God. Whether you are a new believer or have been walking with Christ for years, this devotional offers a chance to grow in faith, find encouragement, and reflect on God's truth for your life. Each chapter is written to meet you where you are, offering biblical insight, practical application, and powerful reminders of God's presence and love.

Life is full of ups and downs, uncertainties and triumphs, but one thing remains constant: God's faithfulness. Through these chapters, you'll discover how to trust Him more fully, embrace His promises, and walk confidently in the purpose He has for you. This is not just a book to read—it's an invitation to experience God in a fresh, personal way.

HOW TO APPROACH THIS DEVOTIONAL

With 52 chapters, this devotional is designed to take you on a yearlong journey if you explore one chapter each week. This format allows you to reflect deeply, meditate on Scripture, and apply the lessons to your daily life. However, you can adapt it to fit your spiritual needs and rhythm.

Here are some suggestions for the best way to go through the devotional:

1. Weekly Reflection
- **Read one chapter per week**: Start by reading the chapter's devotional insight, Scripture focus, and reflection questions early in the week.
- **Meditate throughout the week**: Use the provided Scriptures and practical applications as part of your prayer and study time.
- **Journal your thoughts**: Write down what God is teaching you and how you're applying it in your life.

2. Daily Study Option
- If you prefer a more intensive approach, you can focus on one chapter for several days:
    - **Day 1**: Read the chapter and reflect on the Scripture focus.
    - **Day 2**: Spend time journaling your answers to the reflection questions.

- **Day 3**: Pray through the practical applications, asking God to show you how to implement them.
- **Day 4-5**: Revisit the chapter and focus on how God is speaking to you throughout the week.

3. Thematic Focus

- If a specific chapter resonates with your current season (e.g., Trusting God in Uncertain Times, Strength in Waiting), start there. This devotional is meant to be flexible, allowing you to explore topics that meet you where you are.

4. Group Study

- This devotional can also be used in a small group or Bible study setting:
  - **Weekly meeting**: Discuss one chapter per session, sharing insights, experiences, and how God is working in your lives.
  - **Accountability**: Encourage one another to apply the lessons and pray for each other throughout the week.

A Few Tips to Maximize Your Journey

1. **Start with Prayer**: Before you begin each chapter, ask God to open your heart and guide you into His truth.
2. **Keep a Journal**: Write down your reflections, prayers, and any insights you receive. Over time, this will become a record of how God is working in your life.
3. **Invite the Holy Spirit**: Be attentive to how God may speak to you through Scripture, prayer, or life circumstances as you journey through each chapter.
4. **Go at Your Own Pace**: If you need to pause and spend more time on a chapter, do so. This journey is about transformation, not speed.

5. **Share Your Journey**: Share what you're learning with a friend or family member. Your experiences can inspire and encourage others.

What You'll Discover

Throughout this devotional, you'll uncover themes like:
- Trusting God in every circumstance
- Embracing His grace and forgiveness
- Growing in prayer and faith
- Living with purpose and eternal perspective
- Reflecting His light in a divided and uncertain world

Every chapter is an opportunity to draw closer to God, to know His heart, and to live out the abundant life He's called you to. Whether you're starting fresh or building on years of faith, this journey is a step toward greater intimacy with Him.

A Prayer To Begin

Lord,
Thank You for this opportunity to grow closer to You. As I begin this journey, I ask that You open my heart and guide my steps. Teach me Your truth, transform me with Your Word, and help me to walk in faith and obedience. May this devotional deepen my relationship with You and equip me to live for Your glory. In Jesus' name, I pray. Amen.

MORE THAN CONQUERORS

Romans 8:37

A 52-Week Devotional to Walk in Victory, Faith, and Purpose

PART 1: EMBRACING GOD'S VICTORY

1. **True Freedom in Christ**
2. **Breaking the Chains of Fear**
3. **Trusting God in the Waiting**
4. **Finding Rest for Your Soul**
5. **Overcoming Doubt with Faith**
6. **Finding Joy in the Midst of Trials**
7. **Surrendering Control to God**
8. **The Power of Gratitude**
9. **Walking in Forgiveness**
10. **Embracing God's Peace in the Storm**
11. **Walking by Faith, Not by Sight**
12. **Finding Hope in God's Promises**

PART 2: LIVING WITH PURPOSE AND POWER

13. **Finding Contentment in Every Season**
14. **Overcoming Fear with Faith**
15. **The Gift of God's Grace**
16. **The Joy of Obedience**
17. **Trusting God's Timing**
18. **The Peace That Surpasses Understanding**
19. **Finding Strength in God's Presence**
20. **The Power of Perseverance**
21. **The Blessing of Humility**
22. **Loving Others as Christ Loves Us**
23. **Resting in God's Promises**
24. **Finding Joy in God's Presence**
25. **The Gift of God's Forgiveness**

PART 3: BECOMING MORE LIKE CHRIST

26. **Living in the Power of the Holy Spirit**
27. **Trusting God in the Unknown**
28. **Overcoming the Lies of the Enemy**
29. **The Power of Persistent Prayer**
30. **Living a Life of Gratitude**
31. **Becoming a Vessel of God's Peace**
32. **Strength in Waiting**
33. **Faith That Moves Mountains**
34. **Living in God's Strength**
35. **The Beauty of God's Creation**
36. **Trusting God's Plan**
37. **Walking in the Light of God's Word**

PART 4: WALKING IN THE LIGHT OF ETERNITY

38. **Living a Life of Purpose**
39. **Trusting God in Uncertain Times**
40. **Being a Light in a Divided World**
41. **Equipped for the Battle**
42. **Strength in Fellowship**
43. **Who You Are in Christ**
44. **Walking in Obedience**
45. **The Victory of the Cross**
46. **Living with Eternal Perspective**
47. **Free from Condemnation**
48. **Faithful with What You Have**
49. **The God Who Never Changes**
50. **Finding Joy in Hardships**
51. **The Power of God's Grace**
52. **Starting Fresh: A Journey with Christ (For the New Believer)**

TRUE FREEDOM IN CHRIST

Opening Reflection

We often believe we are free, yet we unknowingly wear the chains of the world around us. These chains are forged by false narratives, misplaced priorities, and worldly distractions that can take hold of our hearts and minds. True freedom isn't found in the fleeting promises of the world but in the eternal truth of Jesus Christ. Today, we'll dive into God's Word to discover what it means to break free from these chains and live in the freedom Christ offers.

Opening Prayer

Heavenly Father,
We come before You with humble hearts, longing to experience the true freedom that only You can provide.

Help us to see the chains that bind us, whether they are fears, worldly influences, or misplaced trust in things outside of You. Open our minds to Your Word, guide our hearts with Your Spirit, and lead us to the truth that sets us free. We ask this in the powerful name of Jesus Christ. Amen.

Scripture Focus

- **John 8:32**: "Then you will know the truth, and the truth will set you free."
- **Romans 12:2**: "Do not conform to the pattern of this world, but be transformed by the renewing of your mind."
- **Colossians 2:8**: "See to it that no one takes you captive through hollow and deceptive philosophy, which depends on human tradition and the elemental spiritual forces of this world rather than on Christ."

Devotional Insight

The world is filled with voices that promise freedom—freedom to do as we please, freedom from accountability, freedom through success or power. But these are not true freedom. In fact, they often lead to greater bondage—chains of anxiety, emptiness, and exhaustion.

Jesus calls us to a different kind of freedom, one that comes from knowing Him and aligning our lives with His truth. This freedom isn't about escaping responsibility or indulging in selfish desires; it's about breaking free from the lies and limitations of the world to embrace the abundant life God has planned for us.

Paul's letter to the Romans challenges us to resist the pull of the world's patterns. Instead, we are called to be transformed by the renewal of our minds—a process that happens when we saturate our hearts with God's Word and seek His guidance in every decision.

When we measure the narratives and philosophies around us against God's truth, we begin to see clearly. No longer will we be swayed by empty promises or hollow ideologies. Instead, we will stand firm in the freedom that comes from knowing Christ.

Reflection Questions

1. What areas of your life feel weighed down or constrained? Are there any "chains" you need to surrender to God?
2. How can you actively renew your mind and guard your heart against the world's false narratives?
3. What does true freedom in Christ mean to you, and how can you embrace it more fully?

Practical Application

- Spend time each day reading scripture that speaks to your identity in Christ. Let His Word be the lens through which you view the world.
- Evaluate the influences in your life—media, relationships, or habits—and ask if they align with God's truth.
- When faced with uncertainty, turn to prayer and scripture for discernment. Trust God to guide your

thoughts and decisions.

Closing Prayer

Lord, we thank You for the freedom You offer through Your Son, Jesus Christ. Help us to see through the lies of the world and walk in the light of Your truth. Break every chain that holds us back from experiencing the abundant life You have planned for us. Teach us to trust in You completely and to stand firm in the freedom You provide. May we live each day transformed by Your Word, renewed by Your Spirit, and anchored in Your love. In Jesus' name, we pray. Amen.

Takeaway Thought

Freedom in Christ is not just the absence of chains—it is the presence of peace, truth, and purpose that comes from living in His light. Let His truth transform you and set you free.

BREAKING THE CHAINS OF FEAR

Opening Reflection

Fear is one of the heaviest chains we carry. It creeps into our minds, paralyzing us, holding us back from God's best, and clouding our faith with doubt. Yet, the Bible tells us repeatedly, "Do not be afraid." God does not call us to live in fear but to walk in courage, trusting in His power and promises. Today, we will explore how to break the chains of fear and replace it with faith.

Opening Prayer

Heavenly Father,
Thank You for being our refuge and strength, an ever-present help in times of trouble. Today, we come to You burdened by fear—fear of the unknown, fear of failure, fear of rejection. Help us to surrender these fears to You and trust in Your perfect love, which casts out all fear. Fill our hearts with courage and peace as we meditate on Your Word and promises. In Jesus' name, we pray. Amen.

Scripture Focus

- **Isaiah 41:10**: "So do not fear, for I am with you; do not be dismayed, for I am your God. I will strengthen you and help you; I will uphold you with my righteous right hand."
- **2 Timothy 1:7**: "For the Spirit God gave us does not make us timid, but gives us power, love, and self-discipline."
- **Psalm 34:4**: "I sought the Lord, and he answered me; he delivered me from all my fears."
- **1 John 4:18**: "There is no fear in love. But perfect love drives out fear, because fear has to do with punishment. The one who fears is not made perfect in love."

Devotional Insight

Fear often feels like a natural response to life's challenges, but it is not what God intended for us. Fear distorts our perspective, magnifying the problems around us while diminishing our trust in God's power. It keeps us bound, preventing us from stepping into the freedom and purpose He has prepared for us.

The Bible is filled with stories of ordinary people who overcame extraordinary fears by trusting in God. Think of Moses, who doubted his ability to lead; of Joshua, who was told multiple times to "be strong and courageous"; or of Peter, who had to summon the courage to step out of the boat and walk on water. In every instance, God's presence and promises were greater than their fear.

God calls us to shift our focus from the things that scare us to the One who saves us. His perfect love drives out fear, reminding us that we are safe in His hands. When we trust Him fully, we find that fear no longer holds the same power over us. Instead,

His Spirit gives us strength, peace, and boldness to walk forward in faith.

Reflection Questions

1. What fears are holding you back from fully trusting God?
2. How can you replace fear with faith in your daily life?
3. In what ways can you remind yourself of God's promises during moments of fear?

Practical Application

- **Name Your Fears**: Write down your fears, then pray over each one, asking God to take them from you and replace them with His peace.
- **Memorize Scripture**: Choose a verse that speaks directly to fear (such as Isaiah 41:10 or Psalm 34:4) and meditate on it daily.
- **Step Out in Faith**: Take one small step toward overcoming a fear. Trust that God will guide and strengthen you as you move forward.

Closing Prayer

Lord, we surrender our fears to You today. Help us to trust in Your power and promises, knowing that You are always with us. Fill our hearts with courage and remind us that Your love casts out all fear. As we step out in faith, may we experience the freedom and joy that comes from walking in obedience to You. Thank You for being our refuge and strength in every situation. In Jesus' name, we pray. Amen.

TRUSTING GOD IN THE WAITING

Opening Reflection

Waiting is one of life's most challenging seasons. Whether you're waiting for an answer, a breakthrough, or healing, the uncertainty can feel overwhelming. Our natural tendency is to seek control, find shortcuts, or grow impatient. Yet, God uses waiting to strengthen our faith, teach us patience, and draw us closer to Him. In the waiting, He is working. Today, we will explore how to trust God in seasons of waiting and embrace His perfect timing.

Opening Prayer

Heavenly Father,
We come to You with hearts that are often restless in seasons of waiting. Teach us to trust You, even when the

path ahead is unclear. Help us to see Your hand at work in the waiting, and remind us that Your timing is perfect. Strengthen our faith, renew our hope, and draw us closer to You as we wait on Your promises. In Jesus' name, we pray. Amen.

Scripture Focus

- **Isaiah 40:31**: "But those who hope in the Lord will renew their strength. They will soar on wings like eagles; they will run and not grow weary, they will walk and not be faint."
- **Psalm 27:14**: "Wait for the Lord; be strong and take heart and wait for the Lord."
- **Lamentations 3:25-26**: "The Lord is good to those whose hope is in him, to the one who seeks him; it is good to wait quietly for the salvation of the Lord."
- **Ecclesiastes 3:11**: "He has made everything beautiful in its time."

Devotional Insight

Waiting feels unnatural because we live in a world of instant gratification. When we're waiting, it can feel like nothing is happening, and we may question if God sees or hears us. However, the Bible assures us that waiting is never wasted when we place our hope in the Lord.

In Isaiah 40:31, we're reminded that waiting on God renews our strength. This isn't passive waiting—it's an active posture of hope and trust. When we lean into God during these seasons, we find that He is faithful to carry us through.

The waiting season is also a refining season. It teaches us to release our desire for control and trust in God's sovereignty. Lamentations 3:25-26 reminds us that God's goodness is revealed as we wait quietly and seek Him. The waiting gives space for our faith to grow and for God's plans to unfold in ways we may not expect.

Ecclesiastes 3:11 reminds us that God's timing is perfect. What may seem delayed to us is right on time in His eternal plan. Trusting God in the waiting requires surrendering our timeline to Him, knowing that He is working all things for our good and His glory.

Reflection Questions

1. Are there areas in your life where you are struggling to trust God's timing?
2. How can you seek God's presence and purpose during a season of waiting?
3. What has God taught you in previous seasons of waiting?

Practical Application

- **Prayer Journaling**: Write down your prayers and concerns during this season of waiting. Reflect on how God is working, even if the answers aren't clear yet.
- **Meditate on Scripture**: Choose a verse about waiting (such as Isaiah 40:31 or Psalm 27:14) and repeat it daily to remind yourself of God's promises.

- **Focus on God's Faithfulness**: Recall past times when you waited on God and how He was faithful to fulfill His promises. Let these memories strengthen your trust.

Closing Prayer

Lord,
Waiting is hard, but we know that You are faithful and Your timing is perfect. Teach us to trust You fully in the waiting, knowing that You are working behind the scenes in ways we cannot see. Help us to find peace in Your presence and strength in Your promises. May we learn patience and grow in faith as we wait on You. Thank You for being a God who never forgets us. We place our hope in You, trusting that all things will be made beautiful in Your time. In Jesus' name, we pray. Amen.

Takeaway Thought

Waiting isn't a delay; it's an opportunity to grow closer to God, trust His timing, and prepare for the beauty He is bringing into your life. Trust Him in the waiting, for He is always faithful.

FINDING REST FOR YOUR SOUL

Opening Reflection

In a world that glorifies busyness, we often feel the weight of constant striving, always moving but never truly at peace. We chase achievements, approval, and solutions to problems, but our hearts remain restless. True rest is not found in the things of this world but in the presence of God. Jesus invites us to lay down our burdens and experience His peace. Today, we'll explore what it means to find rest for your soul in Him.

Opening Prayer

Lord,
We come to You weary and burdened, longing for the rest only You can give. Teach us to release the cares of

this world and place them at Your feet. Quiet our hearts, renew our spirits, and lead us to the peace that comes from trusting fully in You. Help us to embrace Your rest, knowing that in You, our souls can truly find their home. In Jesus' name, we pray. Amen.

Scripture Focus

- **Matthew 11:28-30**: "Come to me, all you who are weary and burdened, and I will give you rest. Take my yoke upon you and learn from me, for I am gentle and humble in heart, and you will find rest for your souls. For my yoke is easy and my burden is light."
- **Psalm 62:1**: "Truly my soul finds rest in God; my salvation comes from him."
- **Exodus 33:14**: "The Lord replied, 'My Presence will go with you, and I will give you rest.'"
- **Isaiah 30:15**: "In repentance and rest is your salvation, in quietness and trust is your strength, but you would have none of it."

Devotional Insight

We often equate rest with inactivity—taking a day off, sitting still, or getting more sleep. While these are important, they cannot restore the deepest parts of us. True rest comes from something greater: surrendering our burdens to Jesus and trusting Him to carry what we cannot.

In Matthew 11:28-30, Jesus gives a beautiful invitation. He calls us to come to Him, not to bring our accomplishments or solutions, but to bring our weariness and burdens. He offers a trade: our heavy yoke for His light one. His rest is not a temporary relief but a deep, abiding peace for our souls.

Many of us resist this rest. We continue to strive, believing that we must solve our problems, fix our lives, or earn God's approval. But Isaiah 30:15 reminds us that rest and trust—not effort—are our strength and salvation. When we slow down and surrender, we create space for God's peace to fill us.

Resting in God doesn't mean we avoid responsibilities; it means we approach them with His strength instead of our own. It's a shift from striving to trusting, from carrying to casting. In this place of rest, we find the renewal and peace our souls long for.

Reflection Questions

1. What burdens are you carrying today that you need to surrender to God?
2. How do you currently define rest? How does God's definition differ?
3. What steps can you take to create space for God's rest in your life?

Practical Application

- **Daily Surrender**: Begin each day with a prayer of surrender, asking God to carry your burdens and guide your steps.
- **Sabbath Rest**: Dedicate one day a week to rest—not just physically but spiritually. Spend time in prayer, worship, and reflection.
- **Create Quiet Moments**: Set aside time each day to sit quietly in God's presence. Let His Word and Spirit renew your soul.

Closing Prayer

Lord,
Thank You for inviting us into Your rest. Help us to stop striving and instead trust in Your strength and promises. Teach us to lay our burdens at Your feet and find peace in Your presence. May we walk each day yoked to You, knowing that You carry what we cannot. Renew our spirits and give us rest for our souls. In Jesus' name, we pray. Amen.

Takeaway Thought

Rest is not found in doing more but in trusting more. Come to Jesus, lay down your burdens, and experience the peace only He can provide.

OVERCOMING DOUBT WITH FAITH

Opening Reflection

Doubt is a natural part of life and faith. It often creeps in during moments of uncertainty, pain, or silence, making us question God's promises and presence. But doubt doesn't have to weaken our faith—it can strengthen it when we bring our questions to God. In today's chapter, we'll explore how to overcome doubt by leaning into God's truth and trusting in His unchanging character.

Opening Prayer

Lord,
Thank You for being patient with us in our doubts. Help

us to bring our questions and uncertainties to You with open hearts, knowing You are faithful to guide us back to Your truth. Strengthen our faith today and remind us that even in our doubt, You remain steadfast. Let Your Word fill us with clarity, hope, and peace. In Jesus' name, we pray. Amen.

Scripture Focus

- **Mark 9:24**: "Immediately the boy's father exclaimed, 'I do believe; help me overcome my unbelief!'"
- **James 1:6**: "But when you ask, you must believe and not doubt, because the one who doubts is like a wave of the sea, blown and tossed by the wind."
- **Hebrews 11:1**: "Now faith is confidence in what we hope for and assurance about what we do not see."
- **Jeremiah 29:13**: "You will seek me and find me when you seek me with all your heart."

Devotional Insight

Doubt can feel isolating, making us wonder if we're failing in our faith. But the Bible shows us that even the strongest believers faced moments of uncertainty. Consider Thomas, who questioned Jesus' resurrection until he saw the scars on His hands. Or Peter, who doubted Jesus' power while walking on water and began to sink. These moments didn't disqualify them —instead, they became opportunities for Jesus to reveal more of Himself and strengthen their faith.

The father in Mark 9:24 gives us a powerful example of honest faith. In his plea, "I do believe; help me overcome my unbelief," we see that doubt and faith can coexist. It's not about having perfect faith but about bringing our doubts to God and trusting

Him to meet us where we are.

When we focus on our doubts, they grow louder. But when we focus on God—His Word, His character, His promises—our faith grows stronger. Hebrews 11:1 reminds us that faith is not about seeing but about trusting. It's about believing in the goodness and sovereignty of God, even when we don't have all the answers.

God doesn't expect us to have it all figured out. He invites us to seek Him, ask questions, and rely on His Spirit to guide us. As we lean into Him, our doubts diminish, and our faith deepens.

Reflection Questions

1. What doubts have you been wrestling with lately?
2. How can you bring those doubts to God and trust Him to guide you through them?
3. Are there areas of your life where you've seen God's faithfulness that can strengthen your faith now?

Practical Application

- **Be Honest with God**: Write down your doubts in a journal and turn them into prayers. Ask God to reveal His truth and strengthen your faith.
- **Anchor in Scripture**: Memorize verses about faith and God's promises (e.g., Hebrews 11:1 or Jeremiah 29:13) to remind yourself of His steadfastness.
- **Seek Community**: Share your doubts with a trusted mentor, pastor, or friend who can encourage you and pray with you.

Closing Prayer

Lord,
Thank You for being a God who welcomes our questions and meets us in our doubt. Help us to bring our uncertainties to You with open hearts, trusting in Your goodness and faithfulness. Strengthen our faith as we meditate on Your Word and remember Your promises. Teach us to focus on You instead of our doubts, knowing that You are always with us and working for our good. In Jesus' name, we pray. Amen.

Takeaway Thought

Doubt isn't the absence of faith—it's an opportunity to deepen it. Bring your questions to God, trust in His promises, and let Him transform your uncertainty into unshakable faith.

FINDING JOY IN THE MIDST OF TRIALS

Opening Reflection

Life's trials often feel overwhelming, stealing our joy and leaving us burdened. Yet, the Bible challenges us to respond to trials with an attitude of joy—not because the difficulties themselves are good, but because they refine our faith and draw us closer to God. True joy doesn't depend on circumstances; it is rooted in the unchanging goodness of God. In this chapter, we'll explore how to find joy in the midst of life's challenges.

Opening Prayer

Heavenly Father,
Thank You for being our source of strength and joy, even in life's hardest moments. Teach us to see beyond our trials and to trust in the work You are doing in and through us. Fill our hearts with Your peace and joy, reminding us that You are always with us. Help us to

focus on Your promises rather than our circumstances. In Jesus' name, we pray. Amen.

Scripture Focus

- **James 1:2-4**: "Consider it pure joy, my brothers and sisters, whenever you face trials of many kinds, because you know that the testing of your faith produces perseverance. Let perseverance finish its work so that you may be mature and complete, not lacking anything."
- **1 Peter 1:6-7**: "In all this you greatly rejoice, though now for a little while you may have had to suffer grief in all kinds of trials. These have come so that the proven genuineness of your faith—of greater worth than gold—may result in praise, glory and honor when Jesus Christ is revealed."
- **Philippians 4:4**: "Rejoice in the Lord always. I will say it again: Rejoice!"
- **Nehemiah 8:10**: "Do not grieve, for the joy of the Lord is your strength."

Devotional Insight

When we face trials, joy may seem like the last thing on our minds. It feels unnatural to rejoice in hardship. However, James 1:2-4 gives us a powerful perspective: trials are not pointless. They test and strengthen our faith, teaching us perseverance and shaping us into the people God has called us to be.

Trials reveal where we've placed our trust. When life feels out of control, we learn to lean on God, who is unchanging. Joy in trials doesn't come from denying the pain but from recognizing that God is using our struggles to refine us. It's about trusting that He is with us and that He will work all things for our good

(Romans 8:28).

The apostle Paul understood this deeply. Writing from prison, he declared in Philippians 4:4, "Rejoice in the Lord always." Paul's joy wasn't rooted in his circumstances but in his relationship with God. He knew that nothing could separate him from God's love, and that truth sustained him.

True joy is a gift from God, fueled by His presence and promises. When we focus on Him rather than our circumstances, we find a joy that cannot be shaken—even in the midst of trials

Reflection Questions

1. How do you usually respond to trials? Is joy a part of your response?
2. What specific challenges are you facing right now that you can surrender to God?
3. How can you focus on God's promises and goodness during difficult times?

Practical Application

- **Shift Your Perspective**: Each time you face a trial, ask, "What might God be teaching me through this?" Pray for wisdom to see the bigger picture.
- **Daily Gratitude**: Keep a gratitude journal, even during trials. Write down three things each day that remind you of God's goodness.
- **Worship in the Storm**: Create a playlist of worship songs that lift your spirit and help you focus on God's faithfulness. Listen to it when you feel overwhelmed.

Closing Prayer

Lord,
Thank You for being our source of joy, even in the hardest seasons of life. Teach us to trust Your plan, knowing that You are refining us through every trial. Help us to see Your goodness and to choose joy, not because our circumstances are easy, but because You are faithful. Strengthen us with Your peace, and remind us that Your joy is our strength. We place our trust in You and rejoice in Your promises. In Jesus' name, we pray. Amen.

Takeaway Thought

Joy is not the absence of trials but the presence of God in the midst of them. Trust in His promises, lean on His strength, and let His joy sustain you through every season.

SURRENDERING CONTROL TO GOD

Opening Reflection

We all desire control—to manage outcomes, plan every detail, and feel secure in knowing what's ahead. Yet, life often reminds us that we are not in control. True peace and freedom come when we surrender our plans, fears, and desires to the One who is sovereign over all. Trusting God with control is not easy, but it is the key to experiencing His perfect peace. Today, we'll explore what it means to let go and let God lead.

Opening Prayer

Heavenly Father,
We confess that we often try to control things that are beyond our reach. Forgive us for holding on too tightly to

our plans and not trusting You fully. Help us to surrender every part of our lives to You, knowing that You are good and Your ways are higher than ours. Teach us to trust Your timing and to rest in Your sovereignty. In Jesus' name, we pray. Amen.

Scripture Focus

- **Proverbs 3:5-6**: "Trust in the Lord with all your heart and lean not on your own understanding; in all your ways submit to him, and he will make your paths straight."
- **Psalm 46:10**: "He says, 'Be still, and know that I am God; I will be exalted among the nations, I will be exalted in the earth.'"
- **Matthew 6:34**: "Therefore do not worry about tomorrow, for tomorrow will worry about itself. Each day has enough trouble of its own."
- **Jeremiah 29:11**: "'For I know the plans I have for you,' declares the Lord, 'plans to prosper you and not to harm you, plans to give you hope and a future.'"

Devotional Insight

Surrendering control is counterintuitive. The world teaches us to plan, prepare, and take charge of our destiny. While planning is wise, we can't control every outcome or predict the future. That's where faith comes in.

Proverbs 3:5-6 calls us to trust God with all our hearts and lean not on our own understanding. This means acknowledging that God's perspective is far greater than ours. He sees the full picture, while we only see a fragment. When we submit to Him, He promises to guide us.

One of the greatest barriers to surrender is fear. We worry

about what might happen if we let go. But Matthew 6:34 reminds us not to be consumed by worry. God cares for the birds of the air and the lilies of the field—how much more does He care for us? When we release control, we make room for His peace to fill our hearts.

Psalm 46:10 invites us to "be still" and recognize God's sovereignty. Stillness is an act of surrender. It's a declaration that we trust God to work things out for our good, even when we can't see the way forward. His plans are always better than ours, and He is faithful to fulfill them in His time.

Reflection Questions

1. What areas of your life are you holding onto tightly and struggling to surrender to God?
2. How has trying to control everything left you feeling overwhelmed or frustrated?
3. What would it look like to fully trust God with your future, your relationships, or your challenges?

Practical Application

- **Prayer of Release**: Take time each day to pray and intentionally release specific worries or plans to God.
- **Meditate on Scripture**: Memorize verses like Proverbs 3:5-6 or Matthew 6:34 to remind yourself of God's sovereignty.
- **Journal Your Surrender**: Write down the areas where you struggle to let go, and note how God moves in

those areas as you surrender them.

Closing Prayer

Lord,
We surrender our plans, our fears, and our desire for control to You. Help us to trust You fully, knowing that You are working all things for our good. Teach us to let go of the things we cannot change and to rest in Your perfect peace. Thank You for being a faithful and loving God, guiding us even when we can't see the way forward. We trust You with every part of our lives. In Jesus' name, we pray. Amen.

Takeaway Thought

Letting go is not losing control—it's giving control to the One who holds the universe in His hands. Surrender your plans to God, trust His timing, and experience the freedom and peace that only He can provide.

THE POWER OF GRATITUDE

Opening Reflection

In the busyness of life, it's easy to focus on what we lack or what's going wrong. Gratitude shifts our perspective, helping us see God's blessings and faithfulness even in difficult times. When we cultivate a heart of gratitude, we draw closer to God and experience joy, peace, and contentment. Today, we'll explore the transformative power of gratitude and how it can shape our relationship with God and others.

Opening Prayer

Father God,
Thank You for the countless blessings You have poured into our lives. Teach us to see Your goodness in every

season and to respond with hearts full of gratitude. Help us to focus on what we have, not what we lack, and to cultivate a spirit of thankfulness in all circumstances. May our gratitude glorify You and draw us closer to Your heart. In Jesus' name, we pray. Amen.

Scripture Focus

- **1 Thessalonians 5:16-18**: "Rejoice always, pray continually, give thanks in all circumstances; for this is God's will for you in Christ Jesus."
- **Psalm 107:1**: "Give thanks to the Lord, for he is good; his love endures forever."
- **Colossians 3:15-17**: "Let the peace of Christ rule in your hearts, since as members of one body you were called to peace. And be thankful. Let the message of Christ dwell among you richly... And whatever you do, whether in word or deed, do it all in the name of the Lord Jesus, giving thanks to God the Father through him."
- **Philippians 4:6-7**: "Do not be anxious about anything, but in every situation, by prayer and petition, with thanksgiving, present your requests to God. And the peace of God, which transcends all understanding, will guard your hearts and your minds in Christ Jesus."

Devotional Insight

Gratitude is more than saying "thank you" or being polite. It's a posture of the heart that acknowledges God's goodness, even in the midst of challenges. 1 Thessalonians 5:16-18 challenges us to give thanks in **all** circumstances—not just when things are going well. This isn't about ignoring pain or pretending struggles don't exist; it's about recognizing that

God's faithfulness and love are constant, no matter what we face.

Gratitude also has a way of shifting our focus. Instead of dwelling on what's wrong, we begin to see God's blessings all around us. Colossians 3:15-17 reminds us to let thankfulness rule in our hearts as a way to invite God's peace and presence into our lives.

Philippians 4:6-7 connects gratitude with prayer and peace. When we bring our requests to God with thanksgiving, we are reminded of His past faithfulness, which strengthens our trust in His future provision. Gratitude doesn't erase our struggles, but it changes how we face them—with faith and confidence in God's goodness.

Gratitude is not just for us; it also glorifies God. Psalm 107:1 calls us to give thanks because of who He is—a good, loving, and faithful Father. When we cultivate a grateful heart, our lives become a testimony of His grace and mercy to those around us.

Reflection Questions

1. What are you grateful for today?
2. How has God shown His faithfulness in your life, even during difficult seasons?
3. What practical steps can you take to cultivate a habit of gratitude in your daily life?

Practical Application

- **Start a Gratitude Journal**: Write down three things you're thankful for every day. Reflect on these blessings during prayer or at the end of the week.
- **Express Thanks to Others**: Take time to thank the people in your life for their kindness, support, or love.

A simple word of gratitude can uplift both you and them.
- **Thank God Daily**: Begin your prayers with thanksgiving. Focus on who God is and the blessings He has given, rather than starting with requests.

Closing Prayer

Lord,
We are so thankful for the many blessings You have given us. Forgive us for the times we've taken them for granted or focused too much on what we don't have. Help us to see Your hand in every part of our lives and to respond with gratitude in all circumstances. Let our hearts overflow with thanksgiving, glorifying You and reminding us of Your faithfulness. May gratitude transform our lives and deepen our relationship with You. In Jesus' name, we pray. Amen.

Takeaway Thought

Gratitude transforms how we see the world and how we experience God's presence. When we focus on His blessings, we discover joy, peace, and contentment—even in the hardest seasons. Choose gratitude today and let it draw you closer to God.

WALKING IN FORGIVENESS

Opening Reflection

Forgiveness is one of the most challenging commands in the Bible. When someone wrongs us, the pain can run deep, and forgiving can feel impossible. Yet, God calls us to forgive, not only for the sake of others but for the sake of our own hearts. Forgiveness is not about condoning what was done—it's about releasing the burden of bitterness and allowing God to bring healing and freedom. Today, we'll explore how to walk in forgiveness, just as God has forgiven us.

Opening Prayer

Father God,
We come to You with hearts that long to be free from the weight of unforgiveness. Help us to reflect on

the forgiveness You have shown us and to extend that same grace to others. Teach us to release our pain and bitterness into Your hands, trusting that You are the ultimate judge and healer. Guide us in walking in forgiveness and experiencing the freedom it brings. In Jesus' name, we pray. Amen.

Scripture Focus

- **Ephesians 4:32**: "Be kind and compassionate to one another, forgiving each other, just as in Christ God forgave you."
- **Matthew 6:14-15**: "For if you forgive other people when they sin against you, your heavenly Father will also forgive you. But if you do not forgive others their sins, your Father will not forgive your sins."
- **Colossians 3:13**: "Bear with each other and forgive one another if any of you has a grievance against someone. Forgive as the Lord forgave you."
- **Romans 12:19**: "Do not take revenge, my dear friends, but leave room for God's wrath, for it is written: 'It is mine to avenge; I will repay,' says the Lord."

Devotional Insight

Forgiveness is at the heart of the gospel. God demonstrated His love for us by forgiving our sins through the sacrifice of Jesus. When we reflect on the depth of God's forgiveness, it gives us the strength and perspective to forgive others, even when it feels impossible.

Forgiveness doesn't mean forgetting what happened or pretending it didn't hurt. It means choosing to release the offense to God and trusting Him to bring justice in His perfect way and timing. Romans 12:19 reminds us that vengeance belongs to God—it is not ours to carry.

Holding onto unforgiveness can feel like power, but it's a trap. Bitterness and resentment poison our hearts, robbing us of peace and joy. Forgiveness, on the other hand, is an act of faith and obedience. It's saying, "God, I trust You to handle this, and I refuse to let this offense define me."

In Matthew 6:14-15, Jesus connects forgiveness with our relationship with God. When we forgive others, we reflect His grace in our own lives. When we hold onto grudges, we block the flow of God's forgiveness and healing. Choosing forgiveness doesn't just set the other person free—it sets us free.

Reflection Questions

1. Is there someone in your life you need to forgive? What is holding you back?
2. How does reflecting on God's forgiveness help you extend forgiveness to others?
3. How can forgiveness lead to healing in your own heart and relationships?

Practical Application

- **Pray for the Person Who Hurt You**: Start by asking God to bless them. This may feel hard, but it helps shift your heart toward forgiveness.
- **Release Bitterness Daily**: Each time negative thoughts about the person arise, intentionally choose to release them to God in prayer.
- **Seek Reconciliation (if Possible)**: If it's safe and appropriate, reach out to the person to rebuild the relationship. If not, release the offense in your heart without requiring their response.

Closing Prayer

Lord,
Thank You for the incredible forgiveness You have shown us through Jesus Christ. Help us to reflect Your grace by forgiving those who have wronged us. Heal the wounds in our hearts and free us from the chains of bitterness and resentment. Teach us to trust You with our pain, knowing that You are the ultimate healer and judge. May we walk in forgiveness and experience the freedom and peace that come from letting go. In Jesus' name, we pray. Amen.

Takeaway Thought

Forgiveness isn't about the person who hurt you—it's about setting your heart free. When you release the offense to God, He replaces the bitterness with His peace and healing. Walk in forgiveness, as He has forgiven you.

EMBRACING GOD'S PEACE IN THE STORM

Opening Reflection

Life's storms often come without warning—unexpected challenges, pain, or loss can leave us feeling shaken and overwhelmed. But even in the midst of chaos, God offers us a peace that surpasses all understanding. His peace doesn't depend on the absence of trouble but on His presence in the middle of it. Today, we'll explore how to embrace God's peace and anchor ourselves in His promises, no matter what storms we face.

Opening Prayer

Father,
Thank You for being our refuge and strength in every season of life. As we face the storms of this world, help us to rest in Your peace and trust in Your unfailing love. Quiet our anxious hearts, calm our restless minds, and

remind us that You are with us. Teach us to look to You and not our circumstances, knowing that You are the one who calms the storm. In Jesus' name, we pray. Amen.

Scripture Focus

- **Philippians 4:6-7**: "Do not be anxious about anything, but in every situation, by prayer and petition, with thanksgiving, present your requests to God. And the peace of God, which transcends all understanding, will guard your hearts and your minds in Christ Jesus."
- **Isaiah 26:3**: "You will keep in perfect peace those whose minds are steadfast, because they trust in you."
- **Mark 4:39-40**: "He got up, rebuked the wind and said to the waves, 'Quiet! Be still!' Then the wind died down and it was completely calm. He said to his disciples, 'Why are you so afraid? Do you still have no faith?'"
- **Psalm 46:1-2**: "God is our refuge and strength, an ever-present help in trouble. Therefore we will not fear, though the earth give way and the mountains fall into the heart of the sea."

Devotional Insight

In Mark 4, the disciples found themselves in a fierce storm while Jesus slept in the boat. They panicked, assuming the worst, but when they woke Jesus, He calmed the storm with just a word: "Quiet! Be still!" Then He asked them, "Why are you so afraid?" This story reminds us that no matter how strong the storm, Jesus is greater. His presence brings peace, even when the waves rage around us.

Philippians 4:6-7 teaches us how to experience this peace. It begins with surrender—bringing our worries to God in prayer and trusting Him to handle what we cannot. God's peace doesn't mean the storm immediately disappears; it means we are guarded by His presence and strengthened by His promises.

Isaiah 26:3 points to the key to perfect peace: steadfast trust in God. When we fix our minds on Him instead of our circumstances, we find a peace that anchors us in the midst of uncertainty. Peace isn't about control—it's about trust.

No matter how fierce the storm, God is our refuge. He promises to be with us, to strengthen us, and to guide us through. When we release our fears to Him, He replaces them with a peace that quiets our souls and calms the storm within us.

Reflection Questions

1. What storms are you currently facing in your life?
2. How can you surrender your worries and anxieties to God today?
3. In what ways have you experienced God's peace in the past, even during difficult times?

Practical Application

- **Start Your Day with Prayer**: Begin each morning by surrendering your worries to God and asking for His peace to guard your heart and mind.
- **Anchor Yourself in Scripture**: Memorize verses like Philippians 4:6-7 or Isaiah 26:3 and repeat them when you feel overwhelmed.
- **Pause and Reflect**: When storms arise, take a moment to pause, breathe, and pray. Remind yourself that God is in control and that He is with you.

Closing Prayer

Lord,
Thank You for being our peace in the midst of life's storms. Help us to trust You fully and to keep our minds fixed on Your promises. When fear and anxiety creep in, remind us that You are with us and that You are greater than any challenge we face. Calm our hearts and fill us with Your perfect peace, no matter what storms come our way. In Jesus' name, we pray. Amen.

Takeaway Thought

God's peace isn't the absence of storms; it's the presence of His power, love, and faithfulness in the midst of them. Trust Him to calm your heart and guide you through every storm.

LIVING WITH PURPOSE

Opening Reflection

Many of us go through life wondering if we are truly making a difference. What is my purpose? Why am I here? God has created each of us uniquely, with specific gifts and a divine purpose. When we align our lives with His plan, we find fulfillment, joy, and a sense of direction. Today, we'll explore what it means to live with purpose and how to walk boldly in the calling God has placed on your life.

Opening Prayer

Father,
Thank You for creating us with intention and purpose. Help us to understand the calling You have placed on our lives and to live in a way that brings glory to You. Give us clarity, courage, and wisdom to use the gifts You have given us to serve others and fulfill Your plan. Guide us to align our hearts with Your will and to trust You in every step of the journey. In Jesus' name, we pray. Amen.

Scripture Focus

- **Jeremiah 29:11**: "For I know the plans I have for you,' declares the Lord, 'plans to prosper you and not to harm you, plans to give you hope and a future."
- **Ephesians 2:10**: "For we are God's handiwork, created in Christ Jesus to do good works, which God prepared in advance for us to do."
- **Proverbs 16:3**: "Commit to the Lord whatever you do, and he will establish your plans."
- **Romans 12:6-8**: "We have different gifts, according to the grace given to each of us. If your gift is prophesying, then prophesy in accordance with your faith; if it is serving, then serve; if it is teaching, then teach; if it is to encourage, then give encouragement; if it is giving, then give generously; if it is to lead, do it diligently; if it is to show mercy, do it cheerfully."

Devotional Insight

God's purpose for your life is not about striving or achieving worldly success—it's about living in alignment with His will. Jeremiah 29:11 reminds us that God's plans are good, filled with hope and a future. Even when we don't see the full picture, we can trust that He is guiding us toward His divine purpose.

Ephesians 2:10 emphasizes that we were created for good works, prepared by God in advance. You are not here by accident; your talents, passions, and experiences were intentionally designed to serve His kingdom. Whether your role seems big or small, every purpose matters in the body of Christ.

Romans 12:6-8 reminds us that God equips us with unique gifts to fulfill His purpose. Whether your gift is teaching, encouraging, serving, or leading, He calls you to use it for His glory. Living with purpose doesn't mean waiting for a grand opportunity—it means faithfully serving where God has placed you today.

Proverbs 16:3 teaches us to commit our plans to the Lord. When we surrender our ambitions and desires to Him, He aligns our hearts with His will, giving us clarity and direction. Purpose is not about what we do—it's about who we serve.

Reflection Questions

1. What gifts or talents has God given you that can be used to serve Him and others?
2. Are there areas of your life where you need to surrender your plans to God?
3. How can you start living with purpose in your daily life, even in small ways?

Practical Application

- **Discover Your Gifts**: Take time to reflect on your talents, passions, and strengths. Pray for God to reveal how He wants you to use them for His glory.
- **Serve Where You Are**: Look for opportunities to serve others in your current season of life, whether at work, in your church, or in your community.
- **Seek God's Guidance**: Regularly pray for wisdom and clarity about your purpose, asking God to align your desires with His will.

Closing Prayer

Lord,
Thank You for creating us with purpose and calling us to live for You. Help us to see the gifts You've given us and to use them faithfully to serve others and bring glory to Your name. Teach us to trust in Your plan, even when we don't see the full picture, and to walk boldly in the purpose You've placed on our lives. May our lives be a reflection of Your love and grace. In Jesus' name, we pray. Amen.

Takeaway Thought

Living with purpose starts with surrendering your plans to God and trusting His direction. Embrace your gifts, serve where you are, and walk confidently in the unique calling He has for your life.

RENEWING YOUR MIND

Opening Reflection

Our thoughts shape our lives. The way we think about ourselves, others, and the world around us has the power to influence our actions and emotions. Too often, our minds are filled with negativity, doubt, or lies that keep us from experiencing the abundant life God desires for us. The Bible calls us to renew our minds by aligning our thoughts with God's truth. Today, we'll explore how to transform our thinking and walk in the freedom of a renewed mind.

Opening Prayer

Father God,
Thank You for giving us Your Word, which renews and restores our minds. Help us to let go of thoughts that do not align with Your truth. Teach us to dwell on what is good, pure, and lovely. Transform our thinking so that we can experience the fullness of life You have for us. May Your Spirit guide us as we seek to align our thoughts with Your will. In Jesus' name, we pray. Amen.

Scripture Focus

- **Romans 12:2**: "Do not conform to the pattern of this world, but be transformed by the renewing of your mind. Then you will be able to test and approve what God's will is—his good, pleasing and perfect will."
- **Philippians 4:8**: "Finally, brothers and sisters, whatever is true, whatever is noble, whatever is right, whatever is pure, whatever is lovely, whatever is admirable—if anything is excellent or praiseworthy—think about such things."
- **2 Corinthians 10:5**: "We demolish arguments and every pretension that sets itself up against the knowledge of God, and we take captive every thought to make it obedient to Christ."
- **Isaiah 26:3**: "You will keep in perfect peace those whose minds are steadfast, because they trust in you."

Devotional Insight

The world is filled with messages that compete for our attention—some are uplifting, but many are not. Romans 12:2 challenges us to resist conforming to the world's patterns of negativity, fear, and sin. Instead, we are called to be transformed by the renewing of our minds, aligning our thoughts with God's truth.

Philippians 4:8 provides a filter for our thoughts. When we focus on what is true, noble, and admirable, we invite God's peace and joy into our lives. Dwelling on God's promises and goodness shifts our perspective, helping us navigate life's challenges with faith and hope.

Renewing our minds also requires intentional action. 2 Corinthians 10:5 reminds us to take every thought captive and make it obedient to Christ. This means replacing lies with truth, rejecting fear with faith, and silencing doubt with the confidence of God's promises.

Isaiah 26:3 reveals the reward of a renewed mind: perfect peace. When our minds are steadfastly focused on God, we experience His peace, no matter the chaos around us. Renewing our minds is not a one-time act but a daily discipline that transforms us from the inside out.

Reflection Questions

1. What thoughts are you holding onto that do not align with God's truth?
2. How can you intentionally focus on what is true, noble, and admirable in your daily life?
3. How does renewing your mind help you draw closer to God and experience His peace?

Practical Application

- **Replace Lies with Truth**: Identify negative or false thoughts and replace them with scripture. For example, replace "I'm not enough" with "I am fearfully and wonderfully made" (Psalm 139:14).
- **Practice Gratitude**: Spend time each day reflecting on God's blessings. Gratitude helps shift your focus to what is good and true.

- **Meditate on Scripture**: Choose a verse like Romans 12:2 or Philippians 4:8 to meditate on throughout the day. Let it guide your thoughts and decisions.

Closing Prayer

Lord,
Thank You for the power of Your Word to renew and transform our minds. Help us to take every thought captive and make it obedient to You. Replace our doubts with faith, our fears with trust, and our negativity with hope. Teach us to focus on what is true and lovely so that we may walk in Your peace and purpose. May our minds be steadfastly fixed on You. In Jesus' name, we pray. Amen.

Takeaway Thought

Renewing your mind is a daily process of aligning your thoughts with God's truth. When you focus on Him, He transforms your thinking, fills you with peace, and equips you to live a life of purpose and joy.

STRENGTH IN WEAKNESS

Opening Reflection

The world tells us that strength comes from self-reliance, power, and control. But God's kingdom operates differently. In His eyes, our weakness is not a flaw—it's an opportunity for His power to shine through us. When we acknowledge our limitations and lean on Him, He gives us the strength to face challenges, fulfill our calling, and grow in faith. Today, we'll explore how God's power is made perfect in our weakness.

Opening Prayer

Father,
We come to You with hearts that feel weak and weary at times. Thank You for reminding us that we don't have to rely on our own strength because Your power is sufficient. Help us to embrace our limitations, trusting that Your grace is enough for every need. Teach us to find strength in You, knowing that Your power is perfected in our weakness. In Jesus' name, we pray. Amen.

Scripture Focus

- **2 Corinthians 12:9-10**: "But he said to me, 'My grace is sufficient for you, for my power is made perfect in weakness.' Therefore I will boast all the more gladly about my weaknesses, so that Christ's power may rest on me. That is why, for Christ's sake, I delight in weaknesses, in insults, in hardships, in persecutions, in difficulties. For when I am weak, then I am strong."
- **Isaiah 40:29-31**: "He gives strength to the weary and increases the power of the weak. Even youths grow tired and weary, and young men stumble and fall; but those who hope in the Lord will renew their strength. They will soar on wings like eagles; they will run and not grow weary, they will walk and not be faint."
- **Philippians 4:13**: "I can do all this through him who gives me strength."
- **Psalm 73:26**: "My flesh and my heart may fail, but God is the strength of my heart and my portion forever."

Devotional Insight

Paul's words in 2 Corinthians 12:9-10 are both humbling and empowering. He doesn't ask God to remove his weakness but instead rejoices in it because it allows Christ's power to rest on him. This is a profound truth: our weaknesses create space for God's strength to be revealed. When we stop striving to be self-sufficient and admit our need for Him, His grace carries us through.

Isaiah 40:29-31 reminds us that God renews the strength of those who trust in Him. Our human strength will always have limits, but God's strength is limitless. When we hope in Him, we can rise above life's challenges with the confidence that He is sustaining us.

Philippians 4:13 is a declaration of faith in God's empowerment. It's not about what we can do on our own but about what we can accomplish when we rely on Him. Similarly, Psalm 73:26 reminds us that even when our bodies and hearts fail, God is our eternal strength and portion.

God doesn't call us to hide our weaknesses. Instead, He invites us to bring them to Him, trusting that His power will work through us. When we do, we experience the freedom of knowing that it's not about our ability—it's about His sufficiency.

Reflection Questions

1. What weaknesses or challenges are you currently facing?
2. How can you invite God's strength into those areas of your life?
3. How does embracing your weakness deepen your faith and reliance on God?

Practical Application

- **Surrender Your Weaknesses**: Write down areas where you feel weak or inadequate. Pray over each one, asking God to work through them.
- **Meditate on God's Strength**: Reflect on verses like 2 Corinthians 12:9-10 or Isaiah 40:29-31 when you feel weary. Let God's promises strengthen you.
- **Celebrate God's Power**: When you see God's strength at work in your weakness, take time to thank Him and share your testimony with others.

Closing Prayer

Lord,
Thank You for reminding us that Your grace is sufficient and Your power is made perfect in our weakness. Help us to stop relying on our own strength and to trust fully in You. Teach us to embrace our limitations as opportunities for Your glory to shine. May we find rest in Your power and joy in knowing that You are always with us. Strengthen our hearts, renew our spirits, and help us to walk in faith. In Jesus' name, we pray. Amen.

Takeaway Thought

Your weakness is not the end—it's an opportunity for God's strength to be revealed. When you surrender your limitations to Him, He will give you the strength to rise above and fulfill His purpose for your life. Trust in His sufficiency today.

THE POWER OF PRAYER

Opening Reflection

Prayer is one of the greatest gifts God has given us. It's our direct line to Him, an intimate conversation with the Creator of the universe. Yet, so often, we underestimate its power. Prayer has the ability to transform our hearts, align us with God's will, and bring about change in the world around us. Today, we'll explore the incredible power of prayer and how it deepens our relationship with God.

Opening Prayer

Heavenly Father,
Thank You for the gift of prayer, for inviting us into Your presence to speak with You freely and openly. Help us

to understand the power of prayer and to approach You with faith and boldness. Teach us to seek Your will in all things and to trust in Your timing and plans. Strengthen our prayer lives and draw us closer to You as we learn to depend on You in every season. In Jesus' name, we pray. Amen.

Scripture Focus

- **Philippians 4:6-7**: "Do not be anxious about anything, but in every situation, by prayer and petition, with thanksgiving, present your requests to God. And the peace of God, which transcends all understanding, will guard your hearts and your minds in Christ Jesus."
- **1 Thessalonians 5:16-18**: "Rejoice always, pray continually, give thanks in all circumstances; for this is God's will for you in Christ Jesus."
- **James 5:16**: "The prayer of a righteous person is powerful and effective."
- **Matthew 6:6**: "But when you pray, go into your room, close the door and pray to your Father, who is unseen. Then your Father, who sees what is done in secret, will reward you."

Devotional Insight

Prayer is more than a ritual or a checklist—it's a lifeline. Philippians 4:6-7 reminds us to bring everything to God in prayer, replacing anxiety with thanksgiving and trust. As we do, God's peace fills our hearts and minds, calming our worries and reminding us of His sovereignty.

1 Thessalonians 5:16-18 challenges us to "pray continually." This doesn't mean spending every waking moment in formal prayer but developing a heart posture of constant

communication with God. When we make prayer a natural part of our daily lives, we draw closer to Him and become more attuned to His voice.

James 5:16 emphasizes the power of prayer to bring about change. Whether we are praying for healing, guidance, or strength, our prayers have impact—not because of our words but because of the One who hears them. Prayer aligns us with God's will and releases His power into our circumstances.

In Matthew 6:6, Jesus teaches us the importance of private, intimate prayer. It's not about impressing others or saying the right words—it's about pouring our hearts out to God and trusting Him to meet us in that sacred space. Prayer isn't about changing God; it's about allowing Him to change us.

Reflection Questions

1. How often do you turn to prayer in your daily life?
2. Are there specific areas of your life where you've seen the power of prayer at work?
3. How can you make prayer a more consistent and intentional part of your routine?

Practical Application

- **Create a Prayer Routine**: Set aside a specific time each day for prayer, whether in the morning, during a break, or before bed.
- **Keep a Prayer Journal**: Write down your prayers and the ways God answers them. Reflecting on His faithfulness will strengthen your faith.
- **Pray for Others**: Make a list of people or situations to pray for regularly. Interceding for others deepens your prayer life and shows God's love in action.

Closing Prayer

Lord,
Thank You for the incredible gift of prayer. Help us to come to You in every situation, trusting in Your power and wisdom. Strengthen our faith as we bring our needs, fears, and hopes before You. Teach us to pray continually, with hearts full of thanksgiving, and to believe in the power of prayer to transform lives. May we draw closer to You each day and glorify You through our prayers. In Jesus' name, we pray. Amen.

Takeaway Thought

Prayer is not just a duty—it's a privilege. It connects us to God's heart, brings peace to our souls, and releases His power into our lives. Make prayer your first response, not your last resort, and watch God move in powerful ways.

WALKING BY FAITH, NOT BY SIGHT

Opening Reflection

Life often presents us with situations that challenge our understanding, leaving us with more questions than answers. In these moments, we're called to walk by faith, trusting in God's unseen plan rather than relying on what we can see. Faith is not about having all the answers—it's about trusting the One who does. Today, we'll explore how to walk confidently by faith, even when the path ahead seems unclear.

Opening Prayer

Father,
Thank You for being faithful and trustworthy in every season of life. Teach us to walk by faith, leaning on Your

promises instead of our own understanding. Help us to trust You fully, even when we cannot see the way forward. Strengthen our faith and remind us that You are always working for our good. In Jesus' name, we pray. Amen.

Scripture Focus

- **2 Corinthians 5:7**: "For we live by faith, not by sight."
- **Hebrews 11:1**: "Now faith is confidence in what we hope for and assurance about what we do not see."
- **Proverbs 3:5-6**: "Trust in the Lord with all your heart and lean not on your own understanding; in all your ways submit to him, and he will make your paths straight."
- **Isaiah 55:8-9**: "'For my thoughts are not your thoughts, neither are your ways my ways,' declares the Lord. 'As the heavens are higher than the earth, so are my ways higher than your ways and my thoughts than your thoughts.'"

Devotional Insight

Faith often requires stepping into the unknown, trusting that God is guiding us even when we don't understand His plan. 2 Corinthians 5:7 reminds us that walking by faith means relying on God's promises rather than our circumstances. It's a call to trust the unseen reality of His presence and His plan.

Hebrews 11:1 defines faith as confidence in what we hope for and assurance about what we do not see. Faith is not blind optimism—it's rooted in the certainty of God's character and His Word. Even when we don't see the full picture, we can trust that God does.

Proverbs 3:5-6 challenges us to submit every part of our lives to God, trusting Him to direct our steps. Walking by faith requires surrendering our need for control and choosing to trust God's wisdom, even when it doesn't align with our understanding.

Isaiah 55:8-9 reminds us that God's ways are higher than ours. His plans are beyond our comprehension, yet they are always good. Faith means trusting that God's perspective is greater than our own, allowing us to rest in His sovereignty even in uncertainty.

Reflection Questions

1. Are there areas of your life where you struggle to trust God's plan?
2. How can you remind yourself of God's faithfulness when you face uncertainty?
3. What steps of faith is God calling you to take today, even if the outcome is unclear?

Practical Application

- **Lean on Scripture**: Meditate on verses like Proverbs 3:5-6 or Hebrews 11:1 when you feel unsure. Let God's Word guide and strengthen your faith.
- **Keep a Faith Journal**: Record times when God has been faithful in the past. Reflect on these moments to encourage your faith in current challenges.
- **Take Small Steps**: Walking by faith doesn't mean you'll always see the whole journey. Start by taking one small step in obedience and trust God to reveal the next.

Closing Prayer

Lord,
Thank You for being a God who is trustworthy, even when we don't understand Your plan. Help us to walk by faith, trusting in Your promises and relying on Your guidance. Teach us to surrender our fears and doubts to You, knowing that You are working all things for our good. Strengthen our confidence in Your Word, and lead us forward in trust and obedience. In Jesus' name, we pray. Amen.

Takeaway Thought

Walking by faith means trusting God even when the way ahead is unclear. His promises are certain, His plans are good, and His love is unfailing. Take the next step in faith, knowing He is guiding you every step of the way.

FINDING HOPE IN GOD'S PROMISES

Opening Reflection

Hope is essential for the human soul, yet life's trials can often leave us feeling hopeless. The good news is that our hope as believers is not rooted in circumstances but in the unshakable promises of God. His Word provides us with an anchor for our souls, reminding us that He is faithful and that His plans are good. Today, we'll explore how to find and hold onto hope in God's promises, even in the darkest seasons.

Opening Prayer

Father,
Thank You for being the source of our hope, even when life feels uncertain. Help us to fix our eyes on Your promises

and trust in Your faithfulness. Teach us to cling to the hope You provide, knowing that You are always working for our good and Your glory. Strengthen our hearts today and fill us with renewed faith in You. In Jesus' name, we pray. Amen.

Scripture Focus

- **Jeremiah 29:11**: "'For I know the plans I have for you,' declares the Lord, 'plans to prosper you and not to harm you, plans to give you hope and a future.'"
- **Romans 15:13**: "May the God of hope fill you with all joy and peace as you trust in him, so that you may overflow with hope by the power of the Holy Spirit."
- **Hebrews 10:23**: "Let us hold unswervingly to the hope we profess, for he who promised is faithful."
- **Isaiah 40:31**: "But those who hope in the Lord will renew their strength. They will soar on wings like eagles; they will run and not grow weary, they will walk and not be faint."

Devotional Insight

Life can feel overwhelming when we focus on our challenges rather than God's promises. Jeremiah 29:11 reminds us that God's plans for us are good, even when we can't see the full picture. His desire is to give us hope and a future, not despair or harm.

Romans 15:13 describes God as the "God of hope." This means that hope is not just a feeling—it's a characteristic of who God is. When we trust in Him, He fills us with joy and peace, allowing us to overflow with hope, not from our own strength but by the power of the Holy Spirit.

Hebrews 10:23 encourages us to hold firmly to our hope

because God is faithful. His promises are sure, and He never fails to keep His Word. No matter what we face, we can trust that He is working behind the scenes to fulfill His purposes.

Isaiah 40:31 reveals that hope in the Lord renews our strength. When we place our hope in Him, we find the endurance and courage to keep going. God's promises are an anchor in the storm, giving us confidence that He will see us through.

Reflection Questions

1. What promises of God bring you the most hope during difficult times?
2. Are there areas in your life where you need to shift your focus from your problems to God's promises?
3. How can you share the hope of God's promises with others who may be struggling?

Practical Application

- **Memorize a Promise**: Choose a scripture that speaks to God's promises and commit it to memory. Repeat it daily to remind yourself of His faithfulness.
- **Hope Journal**: Write down the promises of God that give you hope. Reflect on them during times of discouragement.
- **Encourage Someone**: Share a verse or promise of God with someone who is going through a tough time. Be a light of hope in their life.

Closing Prayer

Lord,
Thank You for the unshakable hope we find in Your promises. When life feels heavy, remind us that You are faithful and that Your plans for us are good. Teach us to trust You more deeply and to hold onto hope, even in the hardest seasons. Fill our hearts with joy and peace as we rest in the assurance of Your Word. Help us to share this hope with others, pointing them to You. In Jesus' name, we pray. Amen.

Takeaway Thought

Hope is not found in circumstances but in the faithfulness of God's promises. When you fix your eyes on Him, you will find strength, peace, and confidence to face whatever lies ahead. Trust in His Word and let hope anchor your soul.

FINDING CONTENTMENT IN EVERY SEASON

Opening Reflection

In a world that constantly pushes us to want more—more success, more possessions, more achievements—it can be hard to feel content. We may believe that contentment will come when circumstances improve, but true contentment isn't found in what we have or where we are. It's found in trusting God and resting in His provision. Today, we'll explore how to cultivate contentment in every season of life, no matter the circumstances.

Opening Prayer

Father,
Thank You for being the ultimate provider of everything
we need. Teach us to find contentment in You, rather than

chasing the fleeting promises of the world. Help us to trust in Your timing, provision, and plan for our lives. Quiet our hearts and fill us with Your peace, so that we may live each day with gratitude and joy. In Jesus' name, we pray. Amen.

Scripture Focus

- **Philippians 4:11-13**: "I am not saying this because I am in need, for I have learned to be content whatever the circumstances. I know what it is to be in need, and I know what it is to have plenty. I have learned the secret of being content in any and every situation, whether well fed or hungry, whether living in plenty or in want. I can do all this through him who gives me strength."
- **1 Timothy 6:6-8**: "But godliness with contentment is great gain. For we brought nothing into the world, and we can take nothing out of it. But if we have food and clothing, we will be content with that."
- **Hebrews 13:5**: "Keep your lives free from the love of money and be content with what you have, because God has said, 'Never will I leave you; never will I forsake you.'"
- **Psalm 37:4**: "Take delight in the Lord, and he will give you the desires of your heart."

Devotional Insight

Paul's words in Philippians 4:11-13 reveal that contentment is a learned skill, not an automatic response. Whether he had much or little, Paul discovered that true contentment comes from relying on God's strength. Contentment is not about ignoring our needs or desires—it's about trusting that God will provide everything we need in His perfect timing.

1 Timothy 6:6 8 reminds us that material possessions are temporary. We enter and leave this world with nothing, but godliness combined with contentment brings lasting satisfaction. When we shift our focus from accumulating things to seeking God, we find joy that the world cannot offer.

Hebrews 13:5 encourages us to live free from the love of money and to be content with what we have. The reason? God is with us. His presence is more valuable than anything we could ever own. When we anchor our contentment in His faithfulness, we experience peace regardless of our circumstances.

Psalm 37:4 invites us to delight in the Lord. When our hearts are aligned with Him, He fulfills our desires—not necessarily by giving us what we want, but by transforming our hearts to desire what He knows is best for us.

Reflection Questions

1. Are there areas in your life where you feel discontent? How can you surrender those to God?
2. How can focusing on God's presence and provision help you cultivate contentment?
3. What steps can you take to delight in the Lord daily, even in challenging seasons?

Practical Application

- **Practice Gratitude**: Each day, write down three things you're thankful for. Focusing on your blessings helps cultivate contentment.
- **Simplify Your Life**: Identify areas where you may be striving for more than you need and choose to live with less, trusting God to meet your needs.
- **Trust in God's Timing**: When you feel discontent, pray for patience and trust that God's plan for you is perfect.

Closing Prayer

Lord,
Thank You for being our provider and sustainer. Teach us to be content in every season, trusting that You are enough. Help us to focus on Your faithfulness rather than the things we lack, and to find joy in Your presence. Transform our hearts so that we desire what You desire, and guide us to live lives of gratitude and peace. In Jesus' name, we pray. Amen.

Takeaway Thought

Contentment is not about having everything you want—it's about trusting that God is everything you need. Rest in His provision, delight in His presence, and let Him teach you the secret of being content in every circumstance.

OVERCOMING FEAR WITH FAITH

Opening Reflection

Fear is a universal experience. Whether it's fear of the unknown, failure, rejection, or loss, it can paralyze us and keep us from living out God's purpose. But God has not called us to live in fear—He has given us a spirit of power, love, and a sound mind. When we place our faith in God, fear loses its grip, and we find the courage to walk boldly in His promises. Today, we'll explore how faith can conquer fear.

Opening Prayer

Lord,
Thank You for being our refuge and strength, a present help in times of trouble. When fear creeps into our

hearts, help us to turn to You, trusting in Your power and promises. Strengthen our faith and remind us that You are always with us, guiding us through every storm. Teach us to walk boldly in faith, knowing that You hold our future in Your hands. In Jesus' name, we pray. Amen.

Scripture Focus

- **2 Timothy 1:7**: "For the Spirit God gave us does not make us timid, but gives us power, love, and self-discipline."
- **Isaiah 41:10**: "So do not fear, for I am with you; do not be dismayed, for I am your God. I will strengthen you and help you; I will uphold you with my righteous right hand."
- **Psalm 34:4**: "I sought the Lord, and he answered me; he delivered me from all my fears."
- **Joshua 1:9**: "Have I not commanded you? Be strong and courageous. Do not be afraid; do not be discouraged, for the Lord your God will be with you wherever you go."

Devotional Insight

Fear often whispers lies: "You're not enough," "You're alone," or "What if everything goes wrong?" But God's Word speaks a louder truth. 2 Timothy 1:7 reminds us that fear is not from God. Instead, He equips us with power, love, and self-discipline to overcome the lies of fear.

Isaiah 41:10 reassures us that we are never alone. God promises to strengthen and uphold us, even in our weakest moments. His presence is our greatest weapon against fear. When we focus on Him rather than our circumstances, fear begins to lose its power.

Psalm 34:4 shows us the power of seeking God in moments of fear. David cried out to the Lord and was delivered—not necessarily from the situation but from the grip of fear. When we surrender our fears to God, He replaces them with His peace.

In Joshua 1:9, God commands us to be strong and courageous. This command is not based on our abilities but on His presence. Knowing that God is with us, we can face any challenge with confidence and faith.

Reflection Questions

1. What fears are holding you back from fully trusting God?
2. How can you replace fearful thoughts with faith-filled truths from God's Word?
3. When have you experienced God's presence giving you courage in a fearful situation?

Practical Application

- **Identify Your Fears**: Write down your fears and then find scriptures that speak directly to them. Pray over those fears, declaring God's truth.
- **Speak God's Promises**: When fear arises, repeat verses like Isaiah 41:10 or 2 Timothy 1:7 aloud to remind yourself of God's power and presence.
- **Take Small Steps**: Choose one fear and take a small step of faith to confront it, trusting that God is with you every step of the way.

Closing Prayer

Lord,
Thank You for Your perfect love that casts out fear. Help

us to surrender our fears to You, trusting that You are bigger than anything we face. Strengthen our faith and fill our hearts with courage, knowing that You are always with us. When fear arises, remind us of Your promises and help us to walk boldly in the truth of who You are. In Jesus' name, we pray. Amen.

Takeaway Thought

Fear may come, but it doesn't have to stay. Faith in God's presence and promises gives you the courage to face any challenge. Trust Him, and let faith triumph over fear.

THE GIFT OF GOD'S GRACE

Opening Reflection

Grace is one of the most beautiful and life-changing gifts from God. It is unearned, undeserved, and freely given. Yet, many of us struggle to fully accept or understand it. We may feel unworthy of God's grace or try to earn His favor through our own efforts. But grace is not about what we do—it's about what Christ has already done for us. Today, we'll explore the transforming power of God's grace and how it sets us free.

Opening Prayer

Father,
Thank You for the incredible gift of Your grace. Help us to understand it more deeply and to embrace it fully.

Teach us to rest in Your love, knowing that we don't have to earn what You've already given freely. Let Your grace transform our hearts and empower us to live for You. In Jesus' name, we pray. Amen.

Scripture Focus

- **Ephesians 2:8-9**: "For it is by grace you have been saved, through faith—and this is not from yourselves, it is the gift of God—not by works, so that no one can boast."
- **2 Corinthians 12:9**: "But he said to me, 'My grace is sufficient for you, for my power is made perfect in weakness.' Therefore I will boast all the more gladly about my weaknesses, so that Christ's power may rest on me."
- **Romans 5:20-21**: "But where sin increased, grace increased all the more, so that, just as sin reigned in death, so also grace might reign through righteousness to bring eternal life through Jesus Christ our Lord."
- **Titus 2:11-12**: "For the grace of God has appeared that offers salvation to all people. It teaches us to say 'No' to ungodliness and worldly passions, and to live self-controlled, upright, and godly lives in this present age."

Devotional Insight

Ephesians 2:8-9 reminds us that salvation is a gift. It's not something we can earn or achieve—it's freely given by God through faith in Jesus Christ. This truth humbles us and removes the pressure of striving to be "good enough" in our own strength.

Paul's words in 2 Corinthians 12:9 reveal another aspect of grace: it's not just about salvation; it's also about daily strength.

God's grace is sufficient for every weakness, every failure, and every struggle. When we rely on His grace, we experience His power in our lives.

Romans 5:20-21 highlights the boundless nature of God's grace. No matter how great our sin, God's grace is greater. This doesn't mean we take grace for granted—it means we live in gratitude and awe of a God who forgives and restores us completely.

Finally, Titus 2:11-12 teaches us that grace transforms us. It not only saves us but also empowers us to live godly lives. Grace is not a license to sin; it's the strength to live in a way that reflects God's love and holiness.

Reflection Questions

1. Do you find it difficult to accept God's grace? Why or why not?
2. How has God's grace strengthened you in moments of weakness?
3. How can you live in a way that reflects the transformative power of grace?

Practical Application

- **Meditate on Grace**: Spend time reading and reflecting on passages about God's grace, such as Ephesians 2:8-9 or 2 Corinthians 12:9. Let these truths sink into your heart.
- **Extend Grace to Others**: Look for opportunities to show grace to someone in your life. Forgive, encourage, or bless them, just as God has done for you.
- **Practice Gratitude**: Thank God daily for His grace in your life. Make a habit of recognizing His unmerited favor in every situation.

Closing Prayer

Lord,
Thank You for Your amazing grace that saves us, strengthens us, and transforms us. Help us to rest in the truth that we are loved and forgiven, not because of what we do but because of who You are. Teach us to rely on Your grace daily and to extend it to others. May Your grace empower us to live lives that glorify You. In Jesus' name, we pray. Amen.

Takeaway Thought

God's grace is more than enough for every moment of your life. It saves, sustains, and transforms you, reminding you that you are deeply loved. Embrace His grace today and let it change you from the inside out.

THE JOY OF OBEDIENCE

Opening Reflection

Obedience to God is often misunderstood as a burden or a list of rules to follow. But in reality, obedience is an act of love and trust. It is through obedience that we align our lives with God's perfect will and experience the joy and peace that comes from walking in His ways. Obedience isn't about perfection—it's about surrendering our hearts to God and trusting that His ways are better than ours. Today, we'll discover the joy that comes from living a life of obedience.

Opening Prayer

Heavenly Father,
Thank You for the gift of Your Word, which guides us in the path of righteousness. Help us to understand that

obedience to You is not a burden but a joy. Teach us to trust Your commands, knowing they are for our good and Your glory. Strengthen our hearts to follow You faithfully and reveal the blessings that come from living in obedience to Your will. In Jesus' name, we pray. Amen.

Scripture Focus

- **John 14:15**: "If you love me, keep my commands."
- **1 John 5:3**: "In fact, this is love for God: to keep his commands. And his commands are not burdensome."
- **Psalm 119:105**: "Your word is a lamp for my feet, a light on my path."
- **Isaiah 1:19**: "If you are willing and obedient, you will eat the good things of the land."

Devotional Insight

Obedience is not about legalism—it's about love. John 14:15 reminds us that obedience flows out of our love for Christ. When we truly love God, our desire is to please Him by following His commands. Obedience becomes a joy, not an obligation.

1 John 5:3 assures us that God's commands are not meant to weigh us down but to guide us into a life of freedom and joy. His commands protect us, provide for us, and lead us into His best for our lives. Obedience is an expression of trust, acknowledging that God knows what is best for us.

Psalm 119:105 describes God's Word as a lamp for our feet. Obedience to His Word illuminates our path, giving us clarity and direction in a confusing world. When we walk in obedience, we avoid pitfalls and experience the blessings of living according to His wisdom.

Isaiah 1:19 promises that willing obedience leads to abundance. This isn't just material provision but the deeper satisfaction of knowing we are walking in step with God. Obedience positions us to receive the fullness of His blessings.

Reflection Questions

1. What areas of your life are hardest to surrender in obedience to God?
2. How can you shift your perspective to see obedience as an act of love rather than duty?
3. What blessings have you experienced from following God's commands in the past?

Practical Application

- **Pray for Guidance**: Ask God to reveal areas of your life where He is calling you to greater obedience. Trust Him to guide you step by step.
- **Start Small**: Focus on one specific area of obedience this week, such as being kind, spending time in His Word, or forgiving someone.
- **Celebrate Obedience**: Reflect on the joy and peace that come from obeying God, and thank Him for the blessings that result.

Closing Prayer

Lord,
Thank You for loving us enough to give us Your commands, which guide us into a life of freedom and joy. Help us to see obedience as a response to Your love, not a burden to bear. Strengthen our hearts to follow You faithfully and to trust that Your ways are better than ours. May our obedience bring glory to Your name and draw us closer to You each day. In Jesus' name, we pray. Amen.

Takeaway Thought

Obedience to God is not about rules—it's about relationship. When we trust and obey Him, we experience His peace, joy, and blessings. Walk in obedience today and discover the joy that comes from living in His will.

TRUSTING GOD'S TIMING

Opening Reflection

One of the hardest things to do is wait on God's timing. We live in a fast-paced world that pushes us to act quickly, but God often works on a different schedule. His timing is always perfect, even when it doesn't match ours. Trusting His timing requires patience, faith, and surrender. Today, we'll explore what it means to rest in God's timing and trust that He is working all things for our good.

Opening Prayer

Father,
Thank You for being a God who sees the bigger picture. Help us to trust Your timing, even when it doesn't align with our plans. Teach us to wait patiently and to trust that You are always working behind the scenes for our good. Strengthen our faith and remind us that Your ways are higher than ours. In Jesus' name, we pray. Amen.

Scripture Focus

- **Ecclesiastes 3:1**: "There is a time for everything, and a season for every activity under the heavens."
- **Isaiah 40:31**: "But those who hope in the Lord will renew their strength. They will soar on wings like eagles; they will run and not grow weary, they will walk and not be faint."
- **Habakkuk 2:3**: "For the revelation awaits an appointed time; it speaks of the end and will not prove false. Though it linger, wait for it; it will certainly come and will not delay."
- **Psalm 27:14**: "Wait for the Lord; be strong and take heart and wait for the Lord."

Devotional Insight

Ecclesiastes 3:1 reminds us that God has ordained a season for everything in our lives. Sometimes we rush to move forward or grow impatient, but His timing is perfect, even when we can't see it. Trusting His timing means believing that He is never late and never early.

Isaiah 40:31 encourages us to place our hope in the Lord while we wait. In doing so, He renews our strength and gives us the endurance to continue. Waiting isn't passive—it's an active trust in God's promises, knowing that He will sustain us.

Habakkuk 2:3 speaks of God's appointed time for His plans to unfold. Even when His promises seem delayed, we are encouraged to wait with faith, trusting that He is always on time. God's delays are not denials—they are opportunities for preparation, growth, and reliance on Him.

Psalm 27:14 calls us to wait with courage and strength. Waiting on God isn't about doing nothing—it's about trusting Him with everything. When we surrender our timelines to Him, we experience His peace and learn to walk in step with His perfect plan.

Reflection Questions

1. What areas of your life are you struggling to trust God's timing?
2. How can you shift your focus from impatience to trusting that God's timing is perfect?
3. What has God taught you during seasons of waiting in the past?

Practical Application

- **Surrender in Prayer**: Each day, bring your plans, desires, and timelines to God in prayer. Ask Him to align your heart with His timing.
- **Memorize Scripture**: Meditate on verses like Psalm 27:14 or Isaiah 40:31 to remind yourself of God's faithfulness while you wait.
- **Practice Patience**: Choose one area of your life where you're tempted to rush ahead, and intentionally slow down, trusting God to lead you.

Closing Prayer

Lord,
Thank You for Your perfect timing in every area of our lives. Help us to trust You fully, even when we don't understand the delays. Teach us patience and faith as we wait for Your plans to unfold. Strengthen our hearts and remind us that Your timing is always for our good and Your glory. May we rest in the assurance that You are in

control. In Jesus' name, we pray. Amen.

Takeaway Thought

God's timing is never wrong. Even when you feel delayed or unsure, trust that He is working in ways you cannot see. Wait on Him with faith, knowing that His plans are always worth the wait.

THE PEACE THAT SURPASSES UNDERSTANDING

Opening Reflection

In a world filled with uncertainty and chaos, finding true peace can seem impossible. But God offers us a peace that is not dependent on our circumstances—a peace that surpasses all understanding. This peace is a gift that comes from trusting in Him and resting in His promises. Today, we'll explore how to embrace God's peace, even in the midst of life's challenges.

Opening Prayer

Father,
Thank You for being the source of perfect peace. When the world feels overwhelming, remind us to turn to You. Teach us to trust in Your promises and rest in Your

presence. Fill our hearts with a peace that surpasses all understanding, and help us to share that peace with those around us. In Jesus' name, we pray. Amen.

Scripture Focus

- **Philippians 4:6-7**: "Do not be anxious about anything, but in every situation, by prayer and petition, with thanksgiving, present your requests to God. And the peace of God, which transcends all understanding, will guard your hearts and your minds in Christ Jesus."
- **John 14:27**: "Peace I leave with you; my peace I give you. I do not give to you as the world gives. Do not let your hearts be troubled and do not be afraid."
- **Isaiah 26:3**: "You will keep in perfect peace those whose minds are steadfast, because they trust in you."
- **Colossians 3:15**: "Let the peace of Christ rule in your hearts, since as members of one body you were called to peace. And be thankful."

Devotional Insight

Philippians 4:6-7 reveals the pathway to peace: surrendering our anxieties to God through prayer and thanksgiving. When we bring our concerns to Him, He replaces our worry with a peace that guards our hearts and minds. This peace isn't based on circumstances; it comes from knowing that God is in control.

In John 14:27, Jesus promises a peace unlike anything the world can offer. The world's peace is temporary and fragile, often tied to external factors. But the peace Jesus gives is eternal, unshaken by life's storms, and rooted in His unchanging presence.

Isaiah 26:3 reminds us that trust in God is the foundation of perfect peace. When we keep our minds focused on Him instead of our problems, we find calm in the midst of chaos. Trusting God means believing that He is working all things for good, even when we don't understand His plan.

Colossians 3:15 encourages us to let Christ's peace rule in our hearts. This means allowing His peace to guide our decisions, calm our fears, and shape our relationships. A heart ruled by Christ's peace is a heart filled with gratitude and love.

Reflection Questions

1. What anxieties or fears do you need to surrender to God today?
2. How can you keep your mind steadfastly focused on God's promises instead of your circumstances?
3. In what ways can you share God's peace with others in your life?

Practical Application

- **Daily Surrender**: Begin each day with prayer, surrendering your worries to God and asking for His peace to guard your heart and mind.
- **Memorize a Promise**: Commit a verse like Philippians 4:6-7 or Isaiah 26:3 to memory. Repeat it to yourself when anxiety arises.
- **Create a Peaceful Space**: Dedicate time to quiet reflection, worship, or reading Scripture to invite God's peace into your day.

Closing Prayer

Lord,
Thank You for offering us a peace that surpasses all understanding. Help us to trust You fully, even when life feels uncertain. Teach us to surrender our worries and fears to You, knowing that You are in control. Fill our hearts with Your peace and guide us to live in harmony with others. May we be a light of peace to those around us, pointing them to Your love and faithfulness. In Jesus' name, we pray. Amen.

Takeaway Thought

God's peace is not the absence of challenges but the presence of His assurance and love. When you trust Him fully, you can experience a peace that the world cannot take away. Rest in Him today and let His peace fill your heart.

FINDING STRENGTH IN GOD'S PRESENCE

Opening Reflection

Life often brings challenges that leave us feeling weak, overwhelmed, or inadequate. In those moments, it's easy to rely on our own strength, only to find it's not enough. But God never intended for us to face life's battles on our own. His presence is our greatest source of strength, providing us with the courage, power, and endurance we need to press on. Today, we'll explore how to draw strength from God's presence and find confidence in His power.

Opening Prayer

Father,
Thank You for always being with us. When we feel weak or unsure, remind us that Your presence is our source of strength. Help us to turn to You for guidance, courage, and endurance in every challenge we face. Teach us to

trust in Your power and not our own, knowing that in You, we have all we need. In Jesus' name, we pray. Amen.

Scripture Focus

- **Psalm 46:1**: "God is our refuge and strength, an ever-present help in trouble."
- **Isaiah 41:10**: "So do not fear, for I am with you; do not be dismayed, for I am your God. I will strengthen you and help you; I will uphold you with my righteous right hand."
- **Exodus 33:14**: "The Lord replied, 'My Presence will go with you, and I will give you rest.'"
- **2 Corinthians 12:9**: "But he said to me, 'My grace is sufficient for you, for my power is made perfect in weakness.' Therefore I will boast all the more gladly about my weaknesses, so that Christ's power may rest on me."

Devotional Insight

Psalm 46:1 paints a powerful picture of God as our refuge and strength, always present in times of trouble. When we face challenges, we can find shelter in His presence and draw from His limitless strength. God is not distant—He is with us, ready to help in every moment of need.

Isaiah 41:10 reminds us that God's presence is a source of courage and assurance. He strengthens and upholds us, carrying us through situations we cannot handle on our own. When we feel overwhelmed, this promise reminds us that we are never alone.

In Exodus 33:14, God promises to go with His people, offering both His presence and His rest. Strength doesn't always mean striving—it often means resting in the assurance that God is in control. When we lean into His presence, we find the peace and renewal we need to keep moving forward.

Paul's words in 2 Corinthians 12:9 reveal a beautiful truth: God's power is made perfect in our weakness. When we admit our need for Him, His grace sustains us and His strength carries us. We don't have to be strong on our own—God's power is sufficient for every weakness.

Reflection Questions

1. In what areas of your life do you feel weak or overwhelmed?
2. How can you intentionally seek God's presence in those moments?
3. How have you experienced God's strength in past challenges?

Practical Application

- **Seek Him in Prayer**: When you feel weak, pause and ask God for His strength and presence. Let His peace fill your heart.
- **Meditate on His Promises**: Reflect on verses like Psalm 46:1 or Isaiah 41:10, reminding yourself of God's faithfulness.
- **Rest in Him**: Instead of striving, take time to rest in God's presence through worship, quiet reflection, or simply sitting in stillness with Him.

Closing Prayer

Lord,
Thank You for being our refuge and strength. When we feel weak or overwhelmed, remind us that Your presence is enough. Help us to rest in Your promises and draw from Your power. Teach us to trust in Your plan and rely on Your grace. Strengthen our hearts today and fill us with the confidence that comes from knowing You are always with us. In Jesus' name, we pray. Amen.

Takeaway Thought

God's presence is your greatest source of strength. When you feel weak, lean into Him, trust His power, and find rest in His unfailing love. His strength is perfect in your weakness.

THE POWER OF PERSEVERANCE

Opening Reflection

Life's journey is filled with challenges, setbacks, and seasons of waiting. It can be tempting to give up when the road ahead feels too hard. But God calls us to persevere, trusting that He is working through every trial to strengthen our faith and fulfill His purposes. Perseverance isn't about relying on our own strength—it's about leaning on God's grace and power to keep moving forward. Today, we'll explore how to persevere with faith, endurance, and hope.

Opening Prayer

Lord,
Thank You for being our strength in times of trial.
Teach us to persevere with faith, trusting that You are

working all things for our good. When we feel weary or discouraged, remind us that Your grace is sufficient and that You never leave us alone. Help us to press on, knowing that You are faithful to complete the work You've started in us. In Jesus' name, we pray. Amen.

Scripture Focus

- **James 1:2-4**: "Consider it pure joy, my brothers and sisters, whenever you face trials of many kinds, because you know that the testing of your faith produces perseverance. Let perseverance finish its work so that you may be mature and complete, not lacking anything."
- **Galatians 6:9**: "Let us not become weary in doing good, for at the proper time we will reap a harvest if we do not give up."
- **Romans 5:3-4**: "Not only so, but we also glory in our sufferings, because we know that suffering produces perseverance; perseverance, character; and character, hope."
- **Hebrews 12:1-2**: "Let us run with perseverance the race marked out for us, fixing our eyes on Jesus, the pioneer and perfecter of faith."

Devotional Insight

James 1:2-4 encourages us to view trials as opportunities for growth. While it's natural to avoid or resent difficulties, God uses them to strengthen our faith and develop perseverance. Trials are not meaningless; they are tools in God's hands to make us mature and complete.

Galatians 6:9 reminds us not to grow weary in doing good. Perseverance requires patience, as the harvest often comes in

God's timing, not ours. The promise is clear: if we don't give up, we will see the fruit of our faithfulness.

Romans 5:3-4 offers a powerful perspective on suffering. It teaches us that perseverance leads to character, and character produces hope. God uses our struggles to shape us into His image and to anchor our hope in Him.

Hebrews 12:1-2 calls us to run with perseverance, keeping our eyes fixed on Jesus. He is both our example and our source of strength. When we focus on Him, we find the endurance to keep going, no matter how hard the race becomes.

Reflection Questions

1. What challenges are you currently facing that require perseverance?
2. How can you shift your perspective to see trials as opportunities for growth?
3. What practical steps can you take to keep your focus on Jesus during difficult seasons?

Practical Application

- **Focus on the Goal**: Write down your long-term spiritual goals and remind yourself of them when you feel discouraged.
- **Lean on God's Strength**: Pray for His strength daily and meditate on verses like James 1:2-4 or Hebrews 12:1-2 to encourage your spirit.
- **Celebrate Small Wins**: Recognize and celebrate even the small steps of progress in your journey. Perseverance is built one step at a time.

Closing Prayer

Lord,
Thank You for giving us the strength to persevere through life's challenges. Help us to trust in Your plan and to see trials as opportunities to grow closer to You. Strengthen our faith and renew our hope as we fix our eyes on Jesus. When we feel weary, remind us that You are with us, guiding us every step of the way. May we run this race with endurance, bringing glory to You in all we do. In Jesus' name, we pray. Amen.

Takeaway Thought

Perseverance is not about avoiding difficulties but about trusting God to sustain you through them. Keep pressing forward, fixing your eyes on Jesus, and trust that He will lead you to victory.

THE BLESSING OF HUMILITY

Opening Reflection

Humility is a virtue that often goes against the grain of our culture, which emphasizes self-promotion and independence. Yet, the Bible teaches us that humility is the pathway to God's blessings and favor. When we humble ourselves before the Lord, we recognize our dependence on Him and allow His grace to work in and through us. Today, we'll explore the beauty and power of humility in our relationship with God and others.

Opening Prayer

Father,
Thank You for teaching us the value of humility. Help us to follow the example of Jesus, who lived a life of

perfect humility and selflessness. Teach us to put others before ourselves and to depend fully on You. May we walk in humility, knowing that You lift up those who humble themselves before You. In Jesus' name, we pray. Amen.

Scripture Focus

- **James 4:10**: "Humble yourselves before the Lord, and he will lift you up."
- **Philippians 2:3-4**: "Do nothing out of selfish ambition or vain conceit. Rather, in humility value others above yourselves, not looking to your own interests but each of you to the interests of the others."
- **Micah 6:8**: "He has shown you, O mortal, what is good. And what does the Lord require of you? To act justly and to love mercy and to walk humbly with your God."
- **1 Peter 5:6-7**: "Humble yourselves, therefore, under God's mighty hand, that he may lift you up in due time. Cast all your anxiety on him because he cares for you."

Devotional Insight

James 4:10 promises that when we humble ourselves before God, He will lift us up. Humility isn't about thinking less of ourselves; it's about thinking more of God and trusting Him to exalt us in His timing. It's an act of surrender, acknowledging that we are dependent on His grace.

Philippians 2:3-4 calls us to imitate Christ's humility by putting others first. True humility shifts our focus from self-centered ambitions to valuing and serving others. It fosters unity, love, and compassion in our relationships.

Micah 6:8 highlights humility as a requirement for walking closely with God. To walk humbly with the Lord is to recognize His greatness and submit to His will. It's about aligning our lives with His purpose, acting justly, and loving mercy.

1 Peter 5:6-7 connects humility with trust. When we humble ourselves under God's mighty hand, we cast our anxieties on Him, trusting that He cares for us. Humility allows us to release control and rest in God's provision and timing.

Reflection Questions

1. In what areas of your life do you struggle with pride or self-reliance?
2. How can you practice putting others before yourself in your daily interactions?
3. What steps can you take to walk humbly with God and trust Him more fully?

Practical Application

- **Serve Others**: Look for opportunities to serve someone in need, putting their interests above your own.
- **Practice Gratitude**: Spend time thanking God for His blessings, acknowledging that all good things come from Him.
- **Release Control**: Identify an area where you've been relying on your own strength, and surrender it to God in prayer, trusting Him to work.

Closing Prayer

Lord,
Thank You for showing us the beauty of humility through the life of Jesus. Help us to lay down our pride and self-reliance and to trust in Your perfect plan. Teach us to walk humbly with You, valuing others above ourselves and relying fully on Your grace. May we find joy and peace in surrendering to You, knowing that You care for us deeply. In Jesus' name, we pray. Amen.

Takeaway Thought

Humility is not a sign of weakness but of strength found in dependence on God. When you humble yourself before Him, He lifts you up and fills your life with His grace and blessings. Walk humbly with Him today.

LOVING OTHERS AS CHRIST LOVES US

Opening Reflection

Love is the foundation of our faith. Jesus demonstrated the ultimate act of love by laying down His life for us, and He calls us to love others in the same way. Loving others as Christ loves us is not always easy—it requires selflessness, patience, and grace. But when we choose to love as He commands, we reflect His character and bring His light into the world. Today, we'll explore what it means to love others with the love of Christ.

Opening Prayer

Father,
Thank You for the perfect love You've shown us through Jesus Christ. Teach us to love others as You have loved

us, with selflessness, patience, and grace. Help us to see others through Your eyes and to reflect Your love in all we do. May our lives be a testimony of Your goodness and mercy. In Jesus' name, we pray. Amen.

Scripture Focus

- **John 13:34-35**: "A new command I give you: Love one another. As I have loved you, so you must love one another. By this everyone will know that you are my disciples, if you love one another."
- **1 Corinthians 13:4-7**: "Love is patient, love is kind. It does not envy, it does not boast, it is not proud. It does not dishonor others, it is not self-seeking, it is not easily angered, it keeps no record of wrongs. Love does not delight in evil but rejoices with the truth. It always protects, always trusts, always hopes, always perseveres."
- **1 John 4:19-21**: "We love because he first loved us. Whoever claims to love God yet hates a brother or sister is a liar. For whoever does not love their brother and sister, whom they have seen, cannot love God, whom they have not seen."
- **Ephesians 4:2**: "Be completely humble and gentle; be patient, bearing with one another in love."

Devotional Insight

In John 13:34-35, Jesus gives us a clear command to love one another as He has loved us. His love is sacrificial, unconditional, and transformative. When we love others in this way, we demonstrate that we are His disciples, drawing others to Him through our actions.

1 Corinthians 13:4-7 defines what Christ-like love looks like. It is patient and kind, forgiving and selfless, protective and

enduring. This kind of love goes beyond feelings—it's a choice we make daily to reflect God's love in our relationships.

1 John 4:19-21 reminds us that our ability to love comes from God. His love fills our hearts and enables us to extend grace, forgiveness, and compassion to others. True love for God is demonstrated in how we love the people around us.

Ephesians 4:2 encourages us to walk in humility, gentleness, and patience, bearing with others in love. Loving others doesn't mean they'll always deserve it, but it means choosing to honor God by showing grace, even when it's difficult.

Reflection Questions

1. Who in your life do you find challenging to love? How can you show them Christ-like love?
2. How can you embody the characteristics of love described in 1 Corinthians 13 in your daily relationships?
3. What steps can you take to let God's love flow through you to others?

Practical Application

- **Start with Prayer**: Ask God to help you love others as He loves you. Pray specifically for those you find difficult to love.
- **Act Intentionally**: Show kindness and patience to someone in your life this week. Small acts of love can make a big difference.
- **Forgive Freely**: If you're holding onto a grudge or bitterness, choose to forgive as Christ has forgiven you.

Closing Prayer

Lord,
Thank You for loving us so deeply and unconditionally. Help us to love others with that same selfless love, reflecting Your heart in our words and actions. Teach us to be patient, kind, and forgiving, even when it's hard. Let Your love flow through us so that others may see You in us and be drawn to Your grace. In Jesus' name, we pray. Amen.

Takeaway Thought

Loving others as Christ loves us is not always easy, but it's what we're called to do. Let His love fill your heart and overflow into every relationship, showing the world the power of His transforming grace.

RESTING IN GOD'S PROMISES

Opening Reflection

In a world full of uncertainty, it's easy to feel restless and overwhelmed. We long for peace and assurance, but often look for it in the wrong places—success, relationships, or control. True rest comes only when we place our trust in the unchanging promises of God. His Word is full of promises that remind us of His faithfulness, love, and provision. Today, we'll explore how to rest in God's promises and find peace in every season of life.

Opening Prayer

Father,
Thank You for the unchanging promises found in Your
Word. Teach us to trust in them fully, even when life feels

uncertain. Help us to rest in the knowledge that You are faithful and that Your plans for us are good. Quiet our hearts today and remind us of the peace and security that comes from trusting in You. In Jesus' name, we pray. Amen.

Scripture Focus

- **Matthew 11:28-30**: "Come to me, all you who are weary and burdened, and I will give you rest. Take my yoke upon you and learn from me, for I am gentle and humble in heart, and you will find rest for your souls. For my yoke is easy and my burden is light."
- **Psalm 62:1-2**: "Truly my soul finds rest in God; my salvation comes from him. Truly he is my rock and my salvation; he is my fortress, I will never be shaken."
- **Joshua 21:45**: "Not one of all the Lord's good promises to Israel failed; every one was fulfilled."
- **2 Corinthians 1:20**: "For no matter how many promises God has made, they are 'Yes' in Christ. And so through him the 'Amen' is spoken by us to the glory of God."

Devotional Insight

In Matthew 11:28-30, Jesus invites us to lay down our burdens and find rest in Him. His promises offer relief from the pressure to do it all on our own. Resting in His promises means trusting that He will carry our burdens and guide us gently through life.

Psalm 62:1-2 reminds us that God is our rock and fortress. In Him, we find unshakable security. No matter how uncertain life may feel, we can rest in the assurance that God is in control.

Joshua 21:45 speaks of God's faithfulness to keep His promises. Not one of His promises failed then, and not one will fail now.

This verse reminds us that we can rely on God to fulfill His Word in His perfect timing.

2 Corinthians 1:20 reveals that all of God's promises are fulfilled in Christ. Through Jesus, we have access to every promise of God—peace, salvation, provision, and eternal life. When we trust in His promises, we glorify Him with our faith.

Reflection Questions

1. What burdens are you carrying that you need to surrender to God?
2. How can trusting in God's promises bring rest to your heart and mind?
3. What promises from God's Word give you the most comfort and peace?

Practical Application

- **Write Down Promises**: Choose a few promises from scripture and write them on cards or sticky notes. Place them where you'll see them daily.
- **Surrender in Prayer**: Each morning, pray and intentionally surrender your worries to God, trusting in His faithfulness.
- **Meditate on Rest**: Spend time in quiet reflection, repeating verses like Matthew 11:28-30 or Psalm 62:1-2 to calm your heart and mind.

Closing Prayer

Lord,
Thank You for Your promises that never fail. Help us to trust in Your Word and to rest in the assurance that You are in control. Teach us to surrender our burdens to You, knowing that You are faithful to provide peace, strength, and guidance. Fill our hearts with Your rest and remind us daily of Your unchanging love. In Jesus' name, we pray. Amen.

Takeaway Thought

Resting in God's promises allows us to release our burdens and embrace His peace. Trust in His faithfulness and let His Word be the anchor that keeps you steady in every season.

FINDING JOY IN GOD'S PRESENCE

Opening Reflection

True joy is not dependent on our circumstances but on our connection to God. The world offers temporary happiness, but the joy found in God's presence is lasting and unshakable. When we draw near to Him, we experience the fullness of His love, peace, and purpose, which fills our hearts with joy. Today, we'll explore how to cultivate joy by living in God's presence every day.

Opening Prayer

Father,
Thank You for the gift of joy that comes from being in

Your presence. Teach us to seek You above all else and to rest in the assurance of Your love and faithfulness. Help us to find joy in who You are, no matter what we face. May Your joy overflow in our lives and draw others closer to You. In Jesus' name, we pray. Amen.

Scripture Focus

- **Psalm 16:11**: "You make known to me the path of life; you will fill me with joy in your presence, with eternal pleasures at your right hand."
- **Nehemiah 8:10**: "Do not grieve, for the joy of the Lord is your strength."
- **John 15:11**: "I have told you this so that my joy may be in you and that your joy may be complete."
- **Philippians 4:4**: "Rejoice in the Lord always. I will say it again: Rejoice!"

Devotional Insight

Psalm 16:11 reminds us that joy is found in God's presence. He shows us the path of life, guiding us into a relationship with Him where our hearts are filled with peace and purpose. When we spend time with God, His joy becomes our strength.

Nehemiah 8:10 teaches that the joy of the Lord strengthens us, especially in challenging times. This joy is not based on external circumstances but on the unchanging character of God. It's a reminder that He is our refuge and sustainer.

In John 15:11, Jesus shares that His joy is meant to be in us, making our joy complete. This joy comes from abiding in Him and living in obedience to His Word. It is a joy that transcends the highs and lows of life.

Philippians 4:4 calls us to rejoice in the Lord always. This isn't about ignoring hardships but choosing to focus on God's goodness and faithfulness. Joy is a discipline that grows as we align our hearts with His presence.

Reflection Questions

1. How can you spend more intentional time in God's presence to experience His joy?
2. What circumstances in your life are currently stealing your joy, and how can you surrender them to God?
3. How can you reflect the joy of the Lord to those around you?

Practical Application

- **Daily Devotion**: Set aside time each day to pray, worship, or read God's Word, inviting His presence into your heart.
- **Gratitude Practice**: List three things you're thankful for each day as a way to focus on God's blessings and cultivate joy.
- **Choose Worship**: When you feel discouraged, turn on worship music and sing praises to God. Let His presence lift your spirit.

Closing Prayer

Lord,
Thank You for the unshakable joy we find in Your presence. Teach us to seek You above all else and to rest in

the assurance of Your love. Help us to rejoice in You, even in difficult times, knowing that Your joy is our strength. Fill our hearts with Your peace and let Your joy overflow into every area of our lives. May we be a light of joy to those around us, pointing them to You. In Jesus' name, we pray. Amen.

Takeaway Thought

Joy is not about what happens around you—it's about who lives within you. Stay close to God, and let His presence fill your heart with lasting joy that no circumstance can take away.

RENEWING YOUR HOPE IN DIFFICULT SEASONS

Opening Reflection

Life's challenges can often leave us feeling discouraged and weary. When the road ahead seems uncertain, it's easy to lose sight of the hope we have in Christ. But even in the darkest seasons, God's promises remain steadfast, and He invites us to place our hope in Him. Today, we'll explore how to renew our hope during difficult times by trusting in God's unchanging faithfulness and His ability to bring beauty out of brokenness.

Opening Prayer

Lord,
Thank You for being the anchor of our hope, even in the midst of life's challenges. When we feel overwhelmed or discouraged, remind us of Your promises and renew our

strength. Help us to trust that You are working all things for good, even when we can't see it. Fill our hearts with hope that sustains us through every season. In Jesus' name, we pray. Amen.

Scripture Focus

- **Romans 15:13**: "May the God of hope fill you with all joy and peace as you trust in him, so that you may overflow with hope by the power of the Holy Spirit."
- **Lamentations 3:22-24**: "Because of the Lord's great love we are not consumed, for his compassions never fail. They are new every morning; great is your faithfulness. I say to myself, 'The Lord is my portion; therefore I will wait for him.'"
- **Psalm 42:11**: "Why, my soul, are you downcast? Why so disturbed within me? Put your hope in God, for I will yet praise him, my Savior and my God."
- **Isaiah 40:31**: "But those who hope in the Lord will renew their strength. They will soar on wings like eagles; they will run and not grow weary, they will walk and not be faint."

Devotional Insight

Romans 15:13 calls God the "God of hope," reminding us that true hope is rooted in Him, not in our circumstances. As we trust Him, His Spirit fills us with joy and peace, allowing hope to overflow in our hearts even during the hardest times.

Lamentations 3:22-24 paints a powerful picture of God's unfailing faithfulness. Even in the midst of suffering, His mercies are new every morning. When we declare that He is our portion, we find hope in His sustaining presence, regardless of our circumstances.

Psalm 42:11 reveals the internal struggle many of us face during difficult seasons. It encourages us to redirect our focus, reminding our hearts to hope in God and praise Him, even when we feel downcast. Choosing to hope in God is an act of faith that lifts our spirits.

Isaiah 40:31 promises renewed strength for those who place their hope in the Lord. When we wait on Him, He equips us to rise above life's challenges with endurance and courage. His strength becomes our source of hope and sustenance.

Reflection Questions

1. What has been stealing your hope lately, and how can you surrender it to God?
2. How can you remind yourself of God's faithfulness during difficult seasons?
3. What practical steps can you take to renew your hope in the Lord today?

Practical Application

- **Daily Reminder**: Write down one of the verses above and place it somewhere you'll see often. Let it remind you of God's promises when you feel discouraged.
- **Focus on Gratitude**: Each evening, reflect on one way God has shown His faithfulness, no matter how small, and thank Him for it.
- **Encourage Others**: Share a word of hope or a scripture with someone else who is going through a difficult time. Encouraging others will strengthen your own hope.

Closing Prayer

Lord,
Thank You for being our source of unshakable hope. When life feels overwhelming, teach us to place our trust in You and to rest in Your promises. Renew our strength and fill us with Your peace, knowing that You are faithful in every season. Help us to share this hope with others, pointing them to Your love and grace. In Jesus' name, we pray. Amen.

Takeaway Thought

Hope in God is the anchor for our souls during life's storms. Trust in His faithfulness, and let His promises renew your hope and strengthen your heart, even in the most difficult seasons.

LIVING A LIFE OF PURPOSE

Opening Reflection

Have you ever wondered why you're here or what God's plan is for your life? Living a life of purpose means aligning your heart, gifts, and actions with God's will. It's not about striving for worldly success but about fulfilling the unique calling God has placed on your life. Today, we'll explore how to discover and live out your God-given purpose, bringing glory to Him and making an eternal impact.

Opening Prayer

Father,
Thank You for creating us with purpose and intention.
Help us to seek Your will for our lives and to trust in

Your guidance. Teach us to use the gifts You've given us to serve others and to glorify You. Open our eyes to the opportunities You've placed before us and give us the courage to walk boldly in the calling You've designed for us. In Jesus' name, we pray. Amen.

Scripture Focus

- **Jeremiah 29:11**: "'For I know the plans I have for you,' declares the Lord, 'plans to prosper you and not to harm you, plans to give you hope and a future.'"
- **Ephesians 2:10**: "For we are God's handiwork, created in Christ Jesus to do good works, which God prepared in advance for us to do."
- **Proverbs 16:9**: "In their hearts humans plan their course, but the Lord establishes their steps."
- **Matthew 5:16**: "In the same way, let your light shine before others, that they may see your good deeds and glorify your Father in heaven."

Devotional Insight

Jeremiah 29:11 reassures us that God's plans for us are good. While we may not always see the full picture, we can trust that He is guiding us toward a hopeful future filled with purpose.

Ephesians 2:10 reminds us that we were created intentionally for good works. Your unique talents, passions, and experiences are not accidental—they are part of God's plan to use you to make a difference in the world.

Proverbs 16:9 highlights the balance between planning and trusting. While it's wise to make plans, we must remain open to God's direction, allowing Him to establish our steps. His plans are always better than ours.

In Matthew 5:16, Jesus calls us to let our light shine. Living a life of purpose means reflecting His love and truth in everything we do, pointing others to Him through our actions and attitudes.

Reflection Questions

1. What gifts, talents, or passions has God given you to serve Him and others?
2. Are there areas of your life where you need to trust God's direction over your own plans?
3. How can you let your light shine in your daily life, bringing glory to God?

Practical Application

- **Discover Your Gifts**: Take time to identify your talents and passions. Pray for God to reveal how you can use them to serve His kingdom.
- **Seek God's Guidance**: Spend intentional time in prayer, asking God to guide your steps and reveal His purpose for you in this season.
- **Impact Others**: Look for one way each day to reflect God's love, whether through kind words, acts of service, or sharing your faith.

Closing Prayer

Lord,
Thank You for creating us with a unique purpose and calling. Help us to seek You daily as we walk in the path You've set before us. Teach us to use our gifts and resources to serve others and to glorify You. Give us the courage to trust Your plans, even when they differ from

our own. Let our lives shine brightly, pointing others to Your love and truth. In Jesus' name, we pray. Amen.

Takeaway Thought

Living a life of purpose means surrendering your plans to God and embracing His calling. Trust Him to guide your steps, use your gifts, and lead you into a life that glorifies Him and impacts others for eternity.

WALKING IN THE LIGHT OF GOD'S TRUTH

Opening Reflection

We live in a world filled with distractions, half-truths, and lies that can lead us away from God's path. Walking in the light of God's truth means allowing His Word to guide us, His Spirit to transform us, and His love to motivate us. When we choose to walk in His light, we reflect His character and illuminate the way for others to know Him. Today, we'll explore how to walk in the light of God's truth and live in alignment with His will.

Opening Prayer

Father,
Thank You for being the light that leads us out of darkness and into truth. Help us to stay rooted in Your Word and to live lives that reflect Your love and holiness.

Teach us to walk in Your light, even when the world pulls us in other directions. May Your truth guide us in every decision and action, bringing glory to Your name. In Jesus' name, we pray. Amen.

Scripture Focus

- **Psalm 119:105**: "Your word is a lamp for my feet, a light on my path."
- **John 8:12**: "When Jesus spoke again to the people, he said, 'I am the light of the world. Whoever follows me will never walk in darkness, but will have the light of life.'"
- **Ephesians 5:8-9**: "For you were once darkness, but now you are light in the Lord. Live as children of light (for the fruit of the light consists in all goodness, righteousness, and truth)."
- **1 John 1:7**: "But if we walk in the light, as he is in the light, we have fellowship with one another, and the blood of Jesus, his Son, purifies us from all sin."

Devotional Insight

Psalm 119:105 reminds us that God's Word is our guide. It illuminates the path before us, giving us clarity and direction when life feels uncertain. Walking in the light of God's truth means consistently turning to His Word for wisdom and guidance.

In John 8:12, Jesus declares Himself the light of the world. When we follow Him, we leave behind the darkness of sin and confusion. His light brings life, clarity, and hope, showing us the way to live in harmony with God's will.

Ephesians 5:8-9 encourages us to live as children of light. This means living in a way that reflects God's goodness, righteousness, and truth. Walking in the light transforms how we think, speak, and act, helping us to be a witness to others.

1 John 1:7 connects walking in the light with fellowship and forgiveness. When we live in the light of God's truth, we experience deeper relationships with others and the ongoing purification of our hearts through Christ's sacrifice.

Reflection Questions

1. Are there areas of your life where you're struggling to walk in the light of God's truth?
2. How can you make God's Word a consistent source of guidance in your daily life?
3. How can your actions reflect God's light to those around you?

Practical Application

- **Daily Scripture Reading**: Spend time each day reading and meditating on God's Word. Let it guide your decisions and shape your perspective.
- **Examine Your Walk**: Reflect on areas where your life may not align with God's truth. Ask Him to reveal any darkness and guide you into His light.
- **Be a Light**: Look for opportunities to reflect God's light by sharing His love, truth, and grace with those around you.

Closing Prayer

Lord,
Thank You for being the light that guides our steps and leads us into truth. Help us to walk faithfully in Your light, leaving behind the darkness of sin and confusion.

Teach us to trust Your Word as our source of wisdom and direction. May our lives reflect Your goodness and bring glory to Your name, drawing others to Your love. In Jesus' name, we pray. Amen.

Takeaway Thought

Walking in God's light means living in truth, love, and righteousness. Let His Word guide you, His Spirit empower you, and His love shine through you as you reflect His light to the world.

FINDING STRENGTH THROUGH SURRENDER

Opening Reflection

Surrendering to God can feel like losing control, but it's actually the path to true strength and freedom. When we try to handle life's burdens on our own, we quickly become weary and overwhelmed. But when we lay everything at God's feet—our plans, struggles, and fears—we invite His power to work in our lives. Today, we'll explore how surrendering to God is the key to finding His strength and peace.

Opening Prayer

Lord,
Thank You for being our refuge and strength. Teach us to let go of our need for control and to trust fully in Your plan. Help us to surrender everything to You—our fears, desires, and burdens—knowing that You are faithful to carry us through. Fill us with Your peace and strength as

we rest in Your promises. In Jesus' name, we pray. Amen.

Scripture Focus

- **Matthew 11:28-30**: "Come to me, all you who are weary and burdened, and I will give you rest. Take my yoke upon you and learn from me, for I am gentle and humble in heart, and you will find rest for your souls. For my yoke is easy and my burden is light."
- **2 Corinthians 12:9-10**: "But he said to me, 'My grace is sufficient for you, for my power is made perfect in weakness.' Therefore I will boast all the more gladly about my weaknesses, so that Christ's power may rest on me. That is why, for Christ's sake, I delight in weaknesses, in insults, in hardships, in persecutions, in difficulties. For when I am weak, then I am strong."
- **Psalm 46:10**: "Be still, and know that I am God; I will be exalted among the nations, I will be exalted in the earth."
- **Proverbs 3:5-6**: "Trust in the Lord with all your heart and lean not on your own understanding; in all your ways submit to him, and he will make your paths straight."

Devotional Insight

Matthew 11:28-30 is an invitation from Jesus to surrender our burdens and take on His yoke—a yoke that is light because He carries it with us. True rest is found not in striving, but in surrendering to Him.

In 2 Corinthians 12:9-10, Paul reminds us that God's grace is sufficient, especially in our weaknesses. Surrendering our struggles allows God's power to be made perfect in us. It's through admitting our need for Him that we find true stren gth.

Psalm 46:10 calls us to be still and acknowledge God's sovereignty. Stillness is an act of surrender, a recognition that we don't have to figure everything out because God is in control.

Proverbs 3:5-6 encourages us to trust God fully, leaning not on our own understanding. When we surrender our plans and decisions to Him, He promises to guide us on the right path.

Reflection Questions

1. What areas of your life are hardest for you to surrender to God?
2. How can surrendering your burdens lead to greater peace and strength?
3. What steps can you take to trust God more fully with your plans and struggles?

Practical Application

- **Surrender in Prayer**: Each day, name specific burdens or worries and release them to God in prayer.
- **Practice Stillness**: Take time each day to sit quietly in God's presence, reflecting on His sovereignty and faithfulness.
- **Lean on Scripture**: Meditate on verses like Matthew 11:28-30 or Proverbs 3:5-6 to remind yourself of God's strength and guidance.

Closing Prayer

Lord,
Thank You for inviting us to surrender our burdens to You. Teach us to let go of our fears and struggles, trusting that You are in control. Help us to rest in Your strength and to rely on Your grace in our weaknesses. Guide us each day as we submit to Your plan, knowing that Your ways are always good. In Jesus' name, we pray. Amen.

Takeaway Thought

Surrender is not a sign of defeat but an act of faith. When you release control and trust God, His strength fills your life, giving you the peace and power to face anything.

THE POWER OF SPEAKING LIFE

Opening Reflection

Our words carry immense power. They can build up or tear down, bring healing or cause pain, inspire faith or sow doubt. As followers of Christ, we are called to speak life—words that reflect God's truth, love, and hope. When we align our speech with His Word, we become vessels of His grace and light to those around us. Today, we'll explore how to harness the power of our words to glorify God and bless others.

Opening Prayer

Father,
Thank You for giving us the gift of words. Teach us to use our speech to build others up and to reflect Your love and

truth. Help us to guard our tongues, choosing words that bring life, healing, and encouragement. Let our words be a testimony of Your goodness and a light in a world that desperately needs hope. In Jesus' name, we pray. Amen.

Scripture Focus

- **Proverbs 18:21**: "The tongue has the power of life and death, and those who love it will eat its fruit."
- **Ephesians 4:29**: "Do not let any unwholesome talk come out of your mouths, but only what is helpful for building others up according to their needs, that it may benefit those who listen."
- **James 3:9-10**: "With the tongue we praise our Lord and Father, and with it we curse human beings, who have been made in God's likeness. Out of the same mouth come praise and cursing. My brothers and sisters, this should not be."
- **Colossians 4:6**: "Let your conversation be always full of grace, seasoned with salt, so that you may know how to answer everyone."

Devotional Insight

Proverbs 18:21 reveals the profound impact of our words. Every word we speak has the potential to bring life or death—to encourage or discourage, to uplift or harm. Being mindful of our words allows us to reflect God's character and offer life to those around us.

Ephesians 4:29 challenges us to use our speech for good, ensuring that our words are helpful, kind, and encouraging. Speaking life doesn't mean avoiding hard truths but delivering them with grace and love, meeting people where they are.

James 3:9-10 reminds us of the inconsistency that can exist in our speech—praising God yet speaking negatively about others. As believers, we are called to use our words for worship and blessing, not harm or division. Our speech should reflect the love of Christ.

Colossians 4:6 calls us to fill our conversations with grace, allowing our words to be "seasoned with salt." This means our speech should preserve and enhance, pointing others to God's goodness while providing wisdom and kindness.

Reflection Questions

1. Do your words consistently reflect God's love and truth, even in challenging situations?
2. Are there times when you've spoken words that hurt others? How can you make amends or change moving forward?
3. How can you intentionally speak life into someone's situation today?

Practical Application

- **Guard Your Tongue**: Before speaking, pause and ask, "Will this word encourage, build up, or glorify God?" If not, consider reframing it.
- **Affirm Someone**: Each day, intentionally speak encouragement or gratitude to someone, highlighting their strengths or God's work in their life.
- **Pray Over Your Words**: Begin your day by asking God to guide your speech, helping you to reflect His grace and love in every conversation.

Closing Prayer

Lord,
Thank You for the power of words to bring life and hope. Help us to use our tongues wisely, speaking truth and love in every situation. Forgive us for the times we've used words to harm rather than heal. Transform our hearts so that our words consistently reflect Your grace and truth. Let everything we say bring glory to Your name and encouragement to others. In Jesus' name, we pray. Amen.

Takeaway Thought

Your words have the power to impact lives for eternity. Speak life, reflect God's love, and let your conversations point others to the hope and truth found in Him.

STANDING FIRM IN FAITH

Opening Reflection

Life's trials and temptations can shake our confidence and test our faith. In those moments, it's easy to feel overwhelmed or uncertain. But God calls us to stand firm, trusting in His promises and relying on His strength. When we build our lives on the solid foundation of Christ, we can withstand any storm. Today, we'll explore how to stand firm in faith, even when life feels unsteady.

Opening Prayer

Father,
Thank You for being our unshakable foundation. Teach

us to stand firm in our faith, no matter what challenges or temptations come our way. Strengthen our hearts and remind us of Your promises, so we can face each day with confidence and courage. Help us to trust in You completely, knowing that You are always with us. In Jesus' name, we pray. Amen.

Scripture Focus

- **1 Corinthians 16:13**: "Be on your guard; stand firm in the faith; be courageous; be strong."
- **Ephesians 6:13**: "Therefore put on the full armor of God, so that when the day of evil comes, you may be able to stand your ground, and after you have done everything, to stand."
- **Psalm 62:6**: "Truly he is my rock and my salvation; he is my fortress, I will not be shaken."
- **Isaiah 41:10**: "So do not fear, for I am with you; do not be dismayed, for I am your God. I will strengthen you and help you; I will uphold you with my righteous right hand."

Devotional Insight

In 1 Corinthians 16:13, Paul calls us to be alert, courageous, and strong as we stand firm in our faith. Faith isn't passive—it requires vigilance and a reliance on God to remain steady in the face of opposition or doubt.

Ephesians 6:13 reminds us to put on the full armor of God. Standing firm isn't about our own strength but about equipping ourselves with His truth, righteousness, peace, faith, and salvation. With God's armor, we are prepared to face any challenge.

Psalm 62:6 highlights God as our rock and fortress. When we

build our faith on His unchanging character, we find stability and peace, no matter how turbulent life becomes. Standing firm means trusting in His power rather than our own.

Isaiah 41:10 offers reassurance that God is with us, strengthening and upholding us. When we feel weak, He provides the courage and support we need to stand firm in His promises.

Reflection Questions

1. What challenges or doubts are shaking your faith right now?
2. How can you put on the armor of God to stand firm in your current season?
3. Who in your life needs encouragement to stand firm in their faith, and how can you support them?

Practical Application

- **Pray for Strength**: Each morning, ask God to give you the strength and courage to stand firm in your faith throughout the day.
- **Equip Yourself**: Study Ephesians 6:10-18 and reflect on how you can actively put on the armor of God in your daily life.
- **Encourage Others**: Share a scripture or word of encouragement with someone who may be struggling

to stand firm in their faith.

Closing Prayer

Lord,
Thank You for being our fortress and strength. Teach us to rely on You fully as we stand firm in faith, no matter what trials or temptations we face. Equip us with Your armor and guide us to live boldly for You. Strengthen our hearts, calm our fears, and help us to trust in Your promises every day. May our faith be a testimony of Your goodness and power. In Jesus' name, we pray. Amen.

Takeaway Thought

Standing firm in faith means trusting God's promises and relying on His strength. When your foundation is in Him, no storm can shake you. Equip yourself with His armor and face each day with courage and confidence.

THE JOY OF SERVING OTHERS

Opening Reflection

Jesus taught us that true greatness is found in serving others. When we serve with a heart of love and humility, we reflect His character and make a lasting impact on the lives of those around us. Serving isn't just about meeting practical needs—it's about showing God's love in action. Today, we'll explore how serving others brings joy, deepens our faith, and glorifies God.

Opening Prayer

Father,
Thank You for the example of Jesus, who came not to be served but to serve. Teach us to follow in His footsteps,

serving others with love, humility, and joy. Help us to see the needs around us and to respond with compassion. May our acts of service glorify You and point others to Your grace. In Jesus' name, we pray. Amen.

Scripture Focus

- **Mark 10:45**: "For even the Son of Man did not come to be served, but to serve, and to give his life as a ransom for many."
- **Galatians 5:13**: "You, my brothers and sisters, were called to be free. But do not use your freedom to indulge the flesh; rather, serve one another humbly in love."
- **Philippians 2:3-4**: "Do nothing out of selfish ambition or vain conceit. Rather, in humility value others above yourselves, not looking to your own interests but each of you to the interests of the others."
- **Matthew 25:40**: "The King will reply, 'Truly I tell you, whatever you did for one of the least of these brothers and sisters of mine, you did for me.'"

Devotional Insight

Mark 10:45 reminds us that Jesus Himself came to serve, not to be served. His ultimate act of service—laying down His life—sets the standard for how we are called to live. Serving others is a reflection of Christ's love and humility.

Galatians 5:13 calls us to use our freedom in Christ to serve one another humbly in love. Serving is not an obligation but a joyful response to the grace we've received. It's an opportunity to extend God's love to those around us.

Philippians 2:3-4 challenges us to value others above ourselves. True service requires humility, putting the needs of others before our own and seeking to bless them without expecting anything in return.

In Matthew 25:40, Jesus teaches that when we serve others, we are serving Him. Acts of kindness and compassion—especially for the least and the marginalized—are seen and treasured by God. Our service becomes an act of worship.

Reflection Questions

1. How can you reflect Christ's love through acts of service in your daily life?
2. Are there areas where you feel hesitant to serve? How can you overcome those hesitations?
3. Who in your life is in need of encouragement or support, and how can you serve them this week?

Practical Application

- **Start Small**: Look for simple ways to serve, like helping a neighbor, encouraging a friend, or volunteering in your community.
- **Serve with Intention**: Pray each morning for God to open your eyes to opportunities to serve and to give you a heart of compassion.
- **Give Without Expectation**: Commit to serving someone this week without expecting anything in return, reflecting the selfless love of Christ.

Closing Prayer

Lord,
Thank You for the privilege of serving others and reflecting Your love. Help us to approach service with joy, humility, and a heart of gratitude. Open our eyes to the needs around us and give us the courage to act. May our service point others to You and bring glory to Your name. Teach us to serve faithfully, as Jesus did, and to find joy in giving of ourselves for Your kingdom. In Jesus' name, we pray. Amen.

Takeaway Thought

Serving others is a powerful way to reflect Christ's love. When you serve with humility and joy, you make an eternal impact and experience the deep satisfaction of living out God's purpose. Look for opportunities to serve today and let God's love shine through you.

FAITH OVER FEAR

Opening Reflection

Fear is a powerful emotion that can paralyze us, cloud our judgment, and cause us to doubt God's promises. But faith invites us to trust God in the face of uncertainty, to believe in His power and goodness even when circumstances seem overwhelming. Today, we'll explore how to replace fear with faith and live with confidence in God's unchanging presence and promises.

Opening Prayer

Father,
Thank You for being our refuge and strength. When fear threatens to take hold, help us to fix our eyes on You and trust in Your unfailing love. Teach us to live by faith, not by sight, and to find courage in Your promises. Strengthen our hearts today and remind us that You are always with us. In Jesus' name, we pray. Amen.

Scripture Focus

- **2 Timothy 1:7**: "For the Spirit God gave us does not make us timid, but gives us power, love, and self-discipline."

- **Isaiah 41:10**: "So do not fear, for I am with you; do not be dismayed, for I am your God. I will strengthen you and help you; I will uphold you with my righteous right hand."
- **Psalm 56:3-4**: "When I am afraid, I put my trust in you. In God, whose word I praise—in God I trust and am not afraid. What can mere mortals do to me?"
- **Joshua 1:9**: "Have I not commanded you? Be strong and courageous. Do not be afraid; do not be discouraged, for the Lord your God will be with you wherever you go."

Devotional Insight

2 Timothy 1:7 reminds us that fear is not from God. He has given us His Spirit, which empowers us with strength, love, and self-control. Faith in Him allows us to step forward boldly, even when fear tries to hold us back.

Isaiah 41:10 offers a powerful reassurance: God is with us, strengthening and helping us in every situation. Fear loses its grip when we remember that we are upheld by His righteous hand.

In Psalm 56:3-4, David demonstrates what it means to choose faith over fear. Instead of allowing fear to dominate, he declares his trust in God. This trust is a deliberate act of faith, rooted in the truth of God's Word.

Joshua 1:9 calls us to be strong and courageous, not because of our own abilities but because of God's presence. When we trust that God is with us, we can face any challenge without fear or discouragement.

Reflection Questions

1. What fears are currently weighing on your heart? How

can you surrender them to God?
2. How has God shown His faithfulness in the past when you've faced fear?
3. What steps can you take to strengthen your faith and trust in God's promises today?

Practical Application

- **Declare Truth**: When fear arises, speak scriptures like Isaiah 41:10 or Joshua 1:9 aloud to remind yourself of God's promises.
- **Pray Through Fear**: Bring your fears to God in prayer, asking Him to replace them with His peace and courage.
- **Take a Bold Step**: Identify one area where fear is holding you back and take a step of faith, trusting God to guide and strengthen you.

Closing Prayer

Lord,
Thank You for Your constant presence and promises that give us courage in the face of fear. Help us to trust in You fully, knowing that You are our refuge and strength. Replace our fears with faith and remind us of Your great love for us. Strengthen us to face every challenge with confidence, knowing that You go before us. In Jesus' name, we pray. Amen.

Takeaway Thought

Faith overcomes fear when we place our trust in God's

presence and promises. He is with you, strengthening and guiding you every step of the way. Choose faith today, and let His courage fill your heart.

THE GIFT OF GOD'S FORGIVENESS

Opening Reflection

Forgiveness is one of the most transformative gifts we receive from God. Through Christ, our sins are not only forgiven but completely erased, allowing us to walk in freedom and peace. This forgiveness is not something we earn—it's a gift of grace. Today, we'll explore how to embrace God's forgiveness, live in its freedom, and extend that same grace to others.

Opening Prayer

Father,
Thank You for the incredible gift of forgiveness through Jesus Christ. Help us to fully accept this gift, letting go

of guilt and shame. Teach us to forgive ourselves, others, and to live in the freedom You've provided. May our lives reflect the grace and mercy we've received. In Jesus' name, we pray. Amen.

Scripture Focus

- **1 John 1:9**: "If we confess our sins, he is faithful and just and will forgive us our sins and purify us from all unrighteousness."
- **Psalm 103:12**: "As far as the east is from the west, so far has he removed our transgressions from us."
- **Ephesians 1:7**: "In him we have redemption through his blood, the forgiveness of sins, in accordance with the riches of God's grace."
- **Colossians 3:13**: "Bear with each other and forgive one another if any of you has a grievance against someone. Forgive as the Lord forgave you."

Devotional Insight

1 John 1:9 reassures us that God's forgiveness is faithful and just. When we confess our sins, we can trust that He not only forgives but purifies us, giving us a fresh start.

Psalm 103:12 beautifully illustrates the completeness of God's forgiveness. He doesn't just forgive—He removes our sins entirely, freeing us from the weight of guilt and shame.

Ephesians 1:7 reminds us that forgiveness is made possible through Christ's sacrifice. His blood redeems us, demonstrating the boundless riches of God's grace and love.

Colossians 3:13 challenges us to extend the forgiveness we've received to others. Forgiveness isn't always easy, but it reflects God's heart and brings healing to relationships.

Reflection Questions

1. Are there sins in your life that you struggle to believe God has forgiven? How can you embrace His grace fully?
2. How can you forgive yourself and let go of guilt, trusting in God's complete forgiveness?
3. Is there someone you need to forgive as an act of obedience and reflection of God's forgiveness?

Practical Application

- **Confess to God**: Spend time in prayer, confessing your sins and thanking Him for His forgiveness and grace.
- **Forgive Yourself**: Write down any areas where you're holding onto guilt or shame. Surrender them to God, trusting in His promise to purify you.
- **Forgive Others**: Identify someone you need to forgive and take a step toward releasing bitterness, even if it's simply through prayer.

Closing Prayer

Lord,
Thank You for forgiving us completely and removing our sins as far as the east is from the west. Help us to live in the freedom of Your forgiveness, letting go of guilt and shame. Teach us to reflect Your grace by forgiving others, even when it's difficult. May our lives be a testimony of Your mercy and love. In Jesus' name, we pray. Amen.

Takeaway Thought

God's forgiveness is a gift of grace that sets us free from guilt and shame. Accept His forgiveness fully, forgive yourself, and extend His grace to others. Live in the freedom of His mercy today.

LIVING IN THE POWER OF THE HOLY SPIRIT

Opening Reflection

The Holy Spirit is a gift given to every believer—a source of power, guidance, and comfort. Through the Spirit, we are equipped to live out our faith, resist temptation, and bear fruit that glorifies God. Yet, many of us struggle to fully rely on His power, often trying to do things in our own strength. Today, we'll explore how to live in the power of the Holy Spirit and allow Him to transform our lives.

Opening Prayer

Father,
Thank You for the gift of the Holy Spirit, who empowers, guides, and strengthens us. Teach us to rely on Him fully, surrendering our own efforts and allowing Your Spirit to work through us. Fill us with Your presence and help us to walk in step with the Spirit every day. In Jesus' name, we

pray. Amen.

Scripture Focus

- **Acts 1:8**: "But you will receive power when the Holy Spirit comes on you; and you will be my witnesses in Jerusalem, and in all Judea and Samaria, and to the ends of the earth."
- **Galatians 5:22-23**: "But the fruit of the Spirit is love, joy, peace, forbearance, kindness, goodness, faithfulness, gentleness, and self-control. Against such things there is no law."
- **Romans 8:11**: "And if the Spirit of him who raised Jesus from the dead is living in you, he who raised Christ from the dead will also give life to your mortal bodies because of his Spirit who lives in you."
- **John 14:26**: "But the Advocate, the Holy Spirit, whom the Father will send in my name, will teach you all things and will remind you of everything I have said to you."

Devotional Insight

Acts 1:8 reminds us that the Holy Spirit empowers us to be witnesses for Christ. His power enables us to share the gospel boldly and live lives that point others to Jesus.

Galatians 5:22-23 reveals the evidence of a Spirit-filled life: the fruit of the Spirit. These qualities—love, joy, peace, and more—are the natural result of allowing the Holy Spirit to transform us from the inside out.

Romans 8:11 speaks to the incredible truth that the same Spirit who raised Jesus from the dead lives in us. This power gives us strength to overcome sin, face challenges, and live victoriously in Christ.

John 14:26 assures us that the Holy Spirit is our Advocate and Teacher. He reminds us of God's Word, provides wisdom, and helps us navigate life with discernment and confidence.

Reflection Questions

1. Are there areas of your life where you're relying on your own strength instead of the power of the Holy Spirit?
2. How can you cultivate the fruit of the Spirit in your daily life?
3. In what ways can you invite the Holy Spirit to guide your decisions and actions?

Practical Application

- **Pray for Guidance**: Begin each day by asking the Holy Spirit to guide you and empower you to live in a way that honors God.
- **Meditate on the Fruit**: Reflect on Galatians 5:22-23 and identify one fruit of the Spirit you want to cultivate more intentionally.
- **Listen for His Voice**: Spend time in quiet prayer or reflection, asking the Holy Spirit to speak to your heart and direct your steps.

Closing Prayer

Lord,
Thank You for the gift of the Holy Spirit, who fills us with power, wisdom, and comfort. Help us to rely on Him daily and to surrender our own efforts to Your strength. Transform our hearts so that we bear the fruit of the Spirit and reflect Your character to the world. Guide us in

every decision and empower us to live boldly for You. In Jesus' name, we pray. Amen.

Takeaway Thought

The Holy Spirit empowers you to live a life that glorifies God. Surrender to His leading, walk in His strength, and let Him transform you into a reflection of Christ's love and power.

TRUSTING GOD IN THE UNKNOWN

Opening Reflection

Life is filled with uncertainties. Whether it's a major life decision, an unexpected challenge, or waiting for clarity, the unknown can feel overwhelming. Yet, God calls us to trust Him, even when we don't see the whole picture. Trusting Him in the unknown isn't easy, but it deepens our faith and brings peace that only He can provide. Today, we'll explore how to rely on God's guidance and promises when the future feels uncertain.

Opening Prayer

Father,
Thank You for being our constant in a world of uncertainties. When life feels unclear, help us to trust in

Your plan and to rest in Your promises. Teach us to rely on Your guidance and to walk by faith, even when we don't know what lies ahead. Fill us with Your peace and remind us that You are always with us. In Jesus' name, we pray. Amen.

Scripture Focus

- **Proverbs 3:5-6**: "Trust in the Lord with all your heart and lean not on your own understanding; in all your ways submit to him, and he will make your paths straight."
- **Isaiah 42:16**: "I will lead the blind by ways they have not known, along unfamiliar paths I will guide them; I will turn the darkness into light before them and make the rough places smooth. These are the things I will do; I will not forsake them."
- **Psalm 46:10**: "Be still, and know that I am God; I will be exalted among the nations, I will be exalted in the earth."
- **Hebrews 11:1**: "Now faith is confidence in what we hope for and assurance about what we do not see."

Devotional Insight

Proverbs 3:5-6 reminds us that trust requires surrender. Instead of leaning on our own understanding, we are called to submit our plans to God, trusting that He will guide us on the right path.

Isaiah 42:16 offers assurance that God leads us through unfamiliar and uncertain places. Even when the path ahead feels dark or rough, He promises to light the way and guide us faithfully.

Psalm 46:10 calls us to be still and trust in God's sovereignty.

When we stop striving to figure everything out and rest in His presence, we discover peace and confidence in His plan.

Hebrews 11:1 highlights the essence of faith: trusting in what we cannot see. Faith in God means believing that He is working all things for good, even when we don't understand how.

Reflection Questions

1. What unknowns or uncertainties are you currently facing?
2. How can you surrender your plans and trust God's guidance in this season?
3. When has God been faithful to guide you through uncertain times in the past?

Practical Application

- **Pray for Trust**: Each day, ask God to strengthen your faith and help you trust Him with the unknown areas of your life.
- **Reflect on His Faithfulness**: Write down past examples of when God has guided you through uncertain times, and use them as reminders of His faithfulness.
- **Take a Step of Faith**: Identify one area where you feel hesitant or unsure and take a small step forward, trusting that God will guide you.

Closing Prayer

Lord,
Thank You for being our guide and comfort in the unknown. Help us to trust You fully, even when we don't see the whole picture. Teach us to rest in Your promises and to walk by faith, not by sight. Strengthen our hearts and remind us that You are always with us, lighting our path and smoothing the way. May we glorify You as we trust in Your perfect plan. In Jesus' name, we pray. Amen.

Takeaway Thought

Trusting God in the unknown is an act of faith and surrender. He knows the path ahead and promises to guide you, even through the darkest and most uncertain times. Rest in His sovereignty and let Him lead.

OVERCOMING THE LIES OF THE ENEMY

Opening Reflection

The enemy works tirelessly to sow seeds of doubt, fear, and insecurity in our hearts. His lies can distort our identity, shake our faith, and keep us from walking in the freedom God has given us. But God has equipped us with the truth of His Word to stand firm and overcome the enemy's schemes. Today, we'll explore how to recognize the lies of the enemy and replace them with the truth of God's promises.

Opening Prayer

Father,
Thank You for giving us Your Word, which is our weapon against the lies of the enemy. Help us to recognize when we are under attack and to stand firm in Your truth. Strengthen our hearts and remind us of who we are in You. Teach us to walk in victory, knowing that Your truth

sets us free. In Jesus' name, we pray. Amen.

Scripture Focus

- **John 8:32**: "Then you will know the truth, and the truth will set you free."
- **2 Corinthians 10:4-5**: "The weapons we fight with are not the weapons of the world. On the contrary, they have divine power to demolish strongholds. We demolish arguments and every pretension that sets itself up against the knowledge of God, and we take captive every thought to make it obedient to Christ."
- **Ephesians 6:11**: "Put on the full armor of God, so that you can take your stand against the devil's schemes."
- **Romans 8:37**: "No, in all these things we are more than conquerors through him who loved us."

Devotional Insight

John 8:32 reminds us that the truth found in God's Word sets us free from the lies of the enemy. When we stand on God's promises, we are no longer bound by fear, shame, or doubt.

In 2 Corinthians 10:4-5, Paul encourages us to take every thought captive and make it obedient to Christ. This means identifying and rejecting any thought that contradicts God's truth, replacing it with His promises.

Ephesians 6:11 calls us to equip ourselves with the full armor of God. This spiritual armor—including the belt of truth and the sword of the Spirit—helps us stand firm against the enemy's schemes.

Romans 8:37 declares that we are more than conquerors through Christ. The enemy may try to deceive us into thinking we are defeated, but God's Word assures us of victory through

His love and power.

Reflection Questions

1. What lies from the enemy have you been believing about yourself, your circumstances, or God?
2. How can you use God's Word to combat those lies and stand firm in His truth?
3. Are you equipping yourself daily with the armor of God to face spiritual battles?

Practical Application

- **Identify the Lies**: Write down any negative or false thoughts you've been struggling with. Then, find scriptures that counteract those lies and meditate on them.
- **Speak Truth Aloud**: When the enemy's lies creep in, declare God's promises out loud as a reminder of His truth.
- **Equip Yourself**: Read Ephesians 6:10-18 and reflect on how you can actively put on the full armor of God each day to stand firm against the enemy.

Closing Prayer

Lord,
Thank You for equipping us with Your Word and the power to stand against the enemy's lies. Help us to recognize when we are under attack and to take every thought captive in obedience to Christ. Strengthen us with Your truth and remind us that we are more than conquerors through Your love. May we walk in victory and freedom, reflecting Your light to the world. In Jesus'

name, we pray. Amen.

Takeaway Thought

The enemy's lies lose their power when we stand on God's truth. Equip yourself with His Word, take every thought captive, and walk confidently in the victory that is already yours in Christ.

THE POWER OF PERSISTENT PRAYER

Opening Reflection

Prayer is one of the most powerful tools God has given us, yet it can often feel challenging to persist when answers don't come immediately. Persistent prayer is not about trying to convince God to act—it's about deepening our relationship with Him and aligning our hearts with His will. Today, we'll explore how to remain steadfast in prayer and trust God's timing and purposes.

Opening Prayer

Father,
Thank You for the gift of prayer and the privilege of coming before You with our needs, hopes, and desires. Teach us to pray with persistence and faith, trusting that You hear us and are working all things for good. Help us to seek You not just for answers but for a deeper relationship

with You. Strengthen our hearts as we wait for Your perfect timing. In Jesus' name, we pray. Amen.

Scripture Focus

- **Luke 18:1**: "Then Jesus told his disciples a parable to show them that they should always pray and not give up."
- **1 Thessalonians 5:16-18**: "Rejoice always, pray continually, give thanks in all circumstances; for this is God's will for you in Christ Jesus."
- **Philippians 4:6**: "Do not be anxious about anything, but in every situation, by prayer and petition, with thanksgiving, present your requests to God."
- **James 5:16**: "The prayer of a righteous person is powerful and effective."

Devotional Insight

In Luke 18:1, Jesus teaches us the importance of persistence in prayer through the parable of the persistent widow. Her unwavering determination is a reminder that God honors the faith of those who continue to seek Him.

1 Thessalonians 5:16-18 encourages us to pray continually, maintaining a spirit of prayer throughout our day. Persistent prayer isn't limited to specific moments; it's an ongoing conversation with God.

Philippians 4:6 reminds us to bring all of our requests to God, offering them with thanksgiving rather than anxiety. Persistent prayer shifts our focus from our worries to God's faithfulness.

James 5:16 emphasizes that prayer is powerful and effective. When we pray persistently, we align ourselves with God's will and invite His power into our lives and circumstances.

Reflection Questions

1. Are there specific prayers you've been tempted to give up on? How can you renew your commitment to pray persistently?
2. How can praying continually deepen your relationship with God?
3. What is one area in your life where you need to trust God's timing and remain steadfast in prayer?

Practical Application

- **Set a Prayer Routine**: Dedicate a specific time each day to bring your requests to God, and remain consistent even when answers seem delayed.
- **Keep a Prayer Journal**: Write down your prayers and revisit them regularly to reflect on God's faithfulness and answered prayers.
- **Pray Throughout the Day**: Develop a habit of short, ongoing prayers in every situation, turning your thoughts toward God in the small and big moments.

Closing Prayer

Lord,
Thank You for always hearing our prayers and inviting us to seek You persistently. Strengthen our faith as we wait for Your answers, trusting in Your perfect timing and wisdom. Help us to remain steadfast in prayer, focusing on You rather than our circumstances. Teach us to find joy and peace in Your presence as we continue to bring our needs and desires before You. In Jesus' name, we pray. Amen.

Takeaway Thought

Persistent prayer is an act of faith and trust in God's timing and purposes. Keep seeking, keep asking, and keep knocking—knowing that God hears you, loves you, and is working for your good.

LIVING A LIFE OF GRATITUDE

Opening Reflection

Gratitude is a powerful practice that shifts our focus from what we lack to what we have been blessed with. It is more than just saying "thank you"—it's a posture of the heart that acknowledges God's goodness in all circumstances. Gratitude transforms our perspective, strengthens our faith, and deepens our relationship with God. Today, we'll explore how to live a life of gratitude, regardless of our circumstances.

Opening Prayer

Father,
Thank You for the countless blessings You've given us, both big and small. Teach us to cultivate a heart of

gratitude that honors You in every season of life. Help us to see Your hand at work, even in the challenges, and to praise You for Your goodness and faithfulness. May our gratitude overflow and inspire others to recognize Your blessings. In Jesus' name, we pray. Amen.

Scripture Focus

- **1 Thessalonians 5:18**: "Give thanks in all circumstances; for this is God's will for you in Christ Jesus."
- **Psalm 107:1**: "Give thanks to the Lord, for he is good; his love endures forever."
- **Colossians 3:17**: "And whatever you do, whether in word or deed, do it all in the name of the Lord Jesus, giving thanks to God the Father through him."
- **Philippians 4:6**: "Do not be anxious about anything, but in every situation, by prayer and petition, with thanksgiving, present your requests to God."

Devotional Insight

1 Thessalonians 5:18 calls us to give thanks in all circumstances—not necessarily for all circumstances but in them. Gratitude is an act of faith that trusts God's goodness even in difficult times.

Psalm 107:1 reminds us that God's goodness and enduring love are reasons to give thanks every day. Gratitude begins with recognizing His unchanging character and faithful provision.

Colossians 3:17 connects gratitude to our daily lives. Whatever we do, whether speaking or acting, can be done with a heart of thankfulness, making every moment an act of worship.

Philippians 4:6 encourages us to pair thanksgiving with our

prayers. Gratitude combats anxiety by shifting our focus from our problems to God's faithfulness and provision.

Reflection Questions

1. What blessings in your life can you thank God for today?
2. How can practicing gratitude help you navigate difficult or uncertain times?
3. In what ways can you express your gratitude to God and to others this week?

Practical Application

- **Gratitude Journal**: Write down three things you're thankful for every day. Reflect on God's blessings and provision.
- **Thank Someone**: Take time to express gratitude to someone who has made a difference in your life. A note, call, or word of thanks can mean a lot.
- **Praise in Prayer**: Start your prayers with thanksgiving, focusing on who God is and what He has done for you before presenting your requests.

Closing Prayer

Lord,
Thank You for the abundant blessings You pour into our lives each day. Help us to see Your hand at work and to give thanks in all circumstances. Teach us to cultivate a heart of gratitude that honors You and reflects Your goodness to others. May our lives be a testimony of thankfulness, bringing glory to Your name. In Jesus' name, we pray. Amen.

Takeaway Thought

Gratitude transforms how we see our circumstances and strengthens our relationship with God. Start each day by focusing on His blessings and let thankfulness shape your heart and your life.

BECOMING A VESSEL OF GOD'S PEACE

Opening Reflection

In a world filled with conflict, stress, and uncertainty, peace can seem elusive. But as followers of Christ, we are called not only to experience God's peace but also to share it with others. Becoming a vessel of God's peace means letting His peace transform us from the inside out and allowing it to overflow into our relationships and communities. Today, we'll explore how to embrace God's peace and share it with the world around us.

Opening Prayer

Father,
Thank You for being the source of true and lasting peace. Fill our hearts with Your peace today, and teach us to reflect it in all that we do. Help us to trust You in every situation and to bring Your peace into the lives of others.

May we be vessels of Your love and light in a world that desperately needs You. In Jesus' name, we pray. Amen.

Scripture Focus

- **Philippians 4:7**: "And the peace of God, which transcends all understanding, will guard your hearts and your minds in Christ Jesus."
- **Matthew 5:9**: "Blessed are the peacemakers, for they will be called children of God."
- **Colossians 3:15**: "Let the peace of Christ rule in your hearts, since as members of one body you were called to peace. And be thankful."
- **Romans 12:18**: "If it is possible, as far as it depends on you, live at peace with everyone."

Devotional Insight

Philippians 4:7 reminds us that God's peace surpasses human understanding. This peace is not dependent on circumstances but flows from our trust in Him. It guards our hearts and minds, giving us strength and stability.

Matthew 5:9 calls us to be peacemakers, reflecting God's heart in a broken world. Peacemaking requires humility, love, and a willingness to build bridges where there is division.

Colossians 3:15 challenges us to let the peace of Christ rule in our hearts. When Christ's peace governs our decisions and interactions, we become agents of His love and unity.

Romans 12:18 emphasizes the importance of striving for peace with others. While we cannot control how others respond, we are responsible for doing everything we can to live at peace with those around us.

Reflection Questions

1. What areas of your life feel unsettled, and how can you invite God's peace into those situations?
2. How can you be a peacemaker in your relationships or community?
3. Are there unresolved conflicts in your life where God is calling you to pursue peace?

Practical Application

- **Seek God's Peace**: Spend time in prayer, asking God to fill your heart with His peace and to help you trust Him in every situation.
- **Resolve Conflicts**: Identify any strained relationships and take steps toward reconciliation, asking God for wisdom and courage.
- **Spread Peace**: Look for opportunities to bring peace into tense situations, whether through kind words, acts of love, or simply being a calming presence.

Closing Prayer

Lord,
Thank You for Your peace that surpasses all understanding. Help us to trust You fully and to let Your peace rule in our hearts. Teach us to be peacemakers in our relationships, our communities, and the world around us. May we reflect Your love and unity, drawing others to You through the peace we share. In Jesus' name, we pray. Amen.

Takeaway Thought

Becoming a vessel of God's peace means letting His peace transform your heart and overflow into the lives of others. Trust Him, pursue peace, and share His love in every interaction.

STRENGTH IN WAITING

Opening Reflection

Waiting is often one of the hardest parts of our journey with God. In seasons of waiting, we may feel restless, discouraged, or even forgotten. But God often uses these times to grow our faith, refine our character, and draw us closer to Him. Waiting is not wasted when we place our hope in God. Today, we'll explore how to find strength in the waiting and trust God's perfect timing.

Opening Prayer

Lord,
Thank You for being with us in every season, including the seasons of waiting. Teach us to trust in Your perfect

timing and to find strength and peace in Your presence. Help us to see the ways You are working in our hearts during the waiting, and remind us that You are always faithful. In Jesus' name, we pray. Amen.

Scripture Focus

- **Isaiah 40:31**: "But those who hope in the Lord will renew their strength. They will soar on wings like eagles; they will run and not grow weary, they will walk and not be faint."
- **Psalm 27:14**: "Wait for the Lord; be strong and take heart and wait for the Lord."
- **Lamentations 3:25**: "The Lord is good to those whose hope is in him, to the one who seeks him."
- **Habakkuk 2:3**: "For the revelation awaits an appointed time; it speaks of the end and will not prove false. Though it linger, wait for it; it will certainly come and will not delay."

Devotional Insight

Isaiah 40:31 reminds us that waiting on the Lord renews our strength. When we place our hope in Him, we find the energy to press on, knowing that He is working on our behalf.

Psalm 27:14 encourages us to take heart and be strong as we wait for the Lord. Waiting is not passive—it's an active posture of faith, trusting that God's plans are worth waiting for.

Lamentations 3:25 highlights God's goodness to those who seek Him. In the waiting, we have the opportunity to deepen our relationship with Him, discovering His faithfulness and love in new ways.

Habakkuk 2:3 assures us that God's promises will be fulfilled at the appointed time. Though it may feel like God's timing is delayed, His plans are never late—they are perfectly aligned with His purposes.

Reflection Questions

1. What are you waiting on God for in this season of your life?
2. How can you shift your perspective to see waiting as a time of growth and preparation?
3. What steps can you take to actively place your hope in God while you wait?

Practical Application

- **Seek God Daily**: Spend intentional time in prayer and Scripture, focusing on God's promises and faithfulness during the waiting.
- **Reflect on His Timing**: Write down past examples of when God's timing proved perfect in your life to remind yourself of His faithfulness.
- **Serve While You Wait**: Look for opportunities to serve others during your waiting season, using the time to reflect God's love and purpose.

Closing Prayer

Lord,
Thank You for the assurance that Your timing is always perfect. Strengthen our hearts as we wait for Your plans to unfold, and help us to trust that You are working behind the scenes. Teach us to rest in Your presence and to embrace the growth and transformation that come during seasons of waiting. May our faith be a testimony

to Your goodness and faithfulness. In Jesus' name, we pray. Amen.

Takeaway Thought

Seasons of waiting are not wasted when we place our hope in God. Trust in His timing, embrace His presence, and let Him renew your strength as you wait for His plans to unfold.

FAITH THAT MOVES MOUNTAINS

Opening Reflection

Faith is powerful. Jesus taught us that even faith as small as a mustard seed can move mountains. This faith isn't about the size of our belief but about the greatness of the God we trust. Mountain-moving faith requires us to step out in confidence, trust God's promises, and believe that nothing is impossible with Him. Today, we'll explore how to cultivate a faith that moves mountains and see God's power at work in our lives.

Opening Prayer

Lord,
Thank You for calling us to live by faith and not by sight. Teach us to trust in Your power and to believe

in Your promises, even when the mountains in our lives feel overwhelming. Strengthen our faith and help us to take bold steps of trust, knowing that You are able to do far more than we can imagine. In Jesus' name, we pray. Amen.

Scripture Focus

- **Matthew 17:20**: "He replied, 'Because you have so little faith. Truly I tell you, if you have faith as small as a mustard seed, you can say to this mountain, 'Move from here to there,' and it will move. Nothing will be impossible for you.'"
- **Mark 11:24**: "Therefore I tell you, whatever you ask for in prayer, believe that you have received it, and it will be yours."
- **Hebrews 11:1**: "Now faith is confidence in what we hope for and assurance about what we do not see."
- **2 Corinthians 5:7**: "For we live by faith, not by sight."

Devotional Insight

Matthew 17:20 emphasizes that faith, even as small as a mustard seed, can accomplish incredible things when it is placed in God. Our faith activates God's power, not because of its size, but because of who we trust.

Mark 11:24 invites us to pray with expectation, believing that God hears and answers our prayers. Faith means trusting that God is working even when we don't see immediate results.

Hebrews 11:1 defines faith as confidence in what we hope for and assurance in what we do not see. Mountain-moving faith requires us to trust in God's promises, even when our circumstances suggest otherwise.

2 Corinthians 5:7 calls us to live by faith and not by sight. Faith challenges us to step forward in obedience, trusting God's power and provision to move the obstacles in our lives.

Reflection Questions

1. What "mountains" are you facing in your life right now that feel impossible to move?
2. How can you trust God's promises and take a step of faith in those areas?
3. What role does prayer play in strengthening your faith and inviting God's power into your situation?

Practical Application

- **Pray Boldly**: Bring your "mountains" to God in prayer, asking Him to intervene and trusting in His power and timing.
- **Take a Step of Faith**: Identify one area in your life where God is calling you to trust Him and take a bold step forward, even if the outcome is uncertain.
- **Meditate on God's Power**: Spend time in Scripture reflecting on stories of God's faithfulness and power, letting them build your confidence in Him.

Closing Prayer

Lord,
Thank You for being the God who moves mountains. Help us to trust in Your power and to believe in Your promises, even when the obstacles before us seem insurmountable. Strengthen our faith and teach us to live by trust in You rather than by what we see. May our lives be a testimony to Your greatness and glory. In Jesus' name, we pray.

Amen.

Takeaway Thought

Faith that moves mountains doesn't depend on your strength but on God's power. Trust Him, pray boldly, and step out in faith, believing that nothing is impossible with Him.

LIVING IN GOD'S STRENGTH

Opening Reflection

Life can often leave us feeling weak, overwhelmed, or unsure of how to move forward. But as believers, we don't have to rely on our own strength to face challenges. God offers His strength to sustain us, equip us, and empower us. When we lean on Him, we discover a power greater than anything we can muster on our own. Today, we'll explore how to rely on God's strength to carry us through every situation.

Opening Prayer

Father,
Thank You for being our source of strength when we feel weak or burdened. Teach us to rely on Your power instead

of our own, and help us to trust in Your ability to sustain us. Fill us with Your Spirit and remind us daily that we can do all things through You. In Jesus' name, we pray. Amen.

Scripture Focus

- **Philippians 4:13**: "I can do all this through him who gives me strength."
- **Isaiah 40:29-31**: "He gives strength to the weary and increases the power of the weak. Even youths grow tired and weary, and young men stumble and fall; but those who hope in the Lord will renew their strength. They will soar on wings like eagles; they will run and not grow weary, they will walk and not be faint."
- **2 Corinthians 12:9**: "But he said to me, 'My grace is sufficient for you, for my power is made perfect in weakness.' Therefore I will boast all the more gladly about my weaknesses, so that Christ's power may rest on me."
- **Psalm 18:32**: "It is God who arms me with strength and keeps my way secure."

Devotional Insight

Philippians 4:13 reminds us that God's strength enables us to face anything that comes our way. This strength isn't about our abilities but about His power working in and through us.

Isaiah 40:29-31 promises renewed strength for those who place their hope in the Lord. When we feel weary or overwhelmed, waiting on God gives us the endurance to keep going and the perspective to rise above our circumstances.

2 Corinthians 12:9 reveals the beauty of God's grace in our weakness. Instead of hiding our struggles, we can bring them to

God, knowing that His power shines brightest when we are at our weakest.

Psalm 18:32 declares that God equips us with the strength we need to stay secure. When we rely on Him, He becomes our foundation, protecting and guiding us through every challenge.

Reflection Questions

1. In what areas of your life are you feeling weak or overwhelmed right now?
2. How can you surrender those areas to God and trust in His strength?
3. What steps can you take to intentionally rely on God's power instead of your own abilities?

Practical Application

- **Pray for Strength**: Begin each day by asking God to give you the strength to face whatever challenges lie ahead.
- **Reflect on His Faithfulness**: Write down times in your life when God provided strength in moments of weakness and let them remind you of His faithfulness.
- **Surrender Your Weaknesses**: Identify areas where you're trying to rely on your own strength, and give them to God in prayer, trusting Him to sustain you.

Closing Prayer

Lord,
Thank You for being our source of strength in every season. When we feel weak, remind us that Your power is made perfect in our weakness. Help us to trust You completely and to rely on Your strength rather than our own. May we find renewed energy and peace in Your

presence, knowing that You will carry us through every challenge. In Jesus' name, we pray. Amen.

Takeaway Thought

God's strength is always available to you. Lean on Him, trust His power, and let His presence sustain you through every challenge and opportunity in life.

THE BEAUTY OF GOD'S CREATION

Opening Reflection

The beauty of creation is one of the ways God reveals Himself to us. From the vastness of the heavens to the intricacy of a single flower, nature declares the glory of its Creator. Taking time to appreciate the beauty of God's handiwork not only reminds us of His greatness but also invites us into a deeper relationship with Him. Today, we'll explore how experiencing God's creation can renew our hearts and strengthen our faith.

Opening Prayer

Father,
Thank You for the beauty of the world You've created.
Help us to see Your hand in every sunrise, every

mountain, and every star. Teach us to pause and reflect on Your greatness and to be reminded of Your love through the wonders of creation. May our hearts overflow with gratitude as we experience the beauty around us. In Jesus' name, we pray. Amen.

Scripture Focus

- **Psalm 19:1**: "The heavens declare the glory of God; the skies proclaim the work of his hands."
- **Romans 1:20**: "For since the creation of the world God's invisible qualities—his eternal power and divine nature—have been clearly seen, being understood from what has been made, so that people are without excuse."
- **Genesis 1:31**: "God saw all that he had made, and it was very good."
- **Isaiah 40:26**: "Lift up your eyes and look to the heavens: Who created all these? He who brings out the starry host one by one and calls forth each of them by name. Because of his great power and mighty strength, not one of them is missing."

Devotional Insight

Psalm 19:1 reminds us that the beauty of the heavens is a reflection of God's glory. Every sunrise, every star, and every cloud points to His majesty and creativity.

Romans 1:20 emphasizes that God's power and divine nature are evident in creation. Observing nature is one way to understand God's greatness and His attention to detail.

Genesis 1:31 declares that all God created was "very good." From the smallest grain of sand to the tallest mountain, every part of creation reflects His perfection and care.

Isaiah 40:26 invites us to look at the heavens and marvel at God's power. He knows each star by name, reminding us of His sovereignty and His intimate knowledge of all He has created.

Reflection Questions

1. How often do you take time to reflect on the beauty of God's creation?
2. In what ways has nature reminded you of God's greatness and love?
3. How can you incorporate moments of awe and gratitude into your daily life as you experience creation?

Practical Application

- **Spend Time in Nature**: Take a walk outside or visit a place where you can observe God's creation. Use this time to pray and reflect on His majesty.
- **Keep a Nature Journal**: Write down things in nature that remind you of God's greatness, such as a beautiful sunset, a bird's song, or the changing seasons.
- **Share Creation's Beauty**: Take a photo of something beautiful in nature and share it with a friend or family member, using it as an opportunity to talk about God's handiwork.

Closing Prayer

Lord,
Thank You for revealing Your glory through the beauty of creation. Help us to pause and marvel at the wonders around us and to see Your hand in every detail. May the beauty of the world You've made draw us closer to You and remind us of Your greatness and love. Teach us to care for Your creation as an act of worship and gratitude. In Jesus' name, we pray. Amen.

Takeaway Thought

God's creation is a reflection of His glory and love. Take time to marvel at the world around you, let it remind you of His greatness, and draw closer to Him through the beauty He has made.

TRUSTING GOD'S PLAN

Opening Reflection

Life often takes unexpected turns, leaving us wondering why things happen the way they do. Trusting God's plan can be difficult, especially when His ways don't align with our expectations. Yet, the Bible reminds us that His plans are always good, and His purposes are far greater than we can imagine. Today, we'll explore how to trust God's plan, even when we don't understand it.

Opening Prayer

Lord,
Thank You for being a God who is always in control,

even when life feels uncertain. Help us to trust Your plan and to surrender our desires and expectations to You. Teach us to rely on Your wisdom and to have faith in Your perfect timing. Give us peace as we trust that You are working all things for good. In Jesus' name, we pray. Amen.

Scripture Focus

- **Jeremiah 29:11**: "'For I know the plans I have for you,' declares the Lord, 'plans to prosper you and not to harm you, plans to give you hope and a future.'"
- **Proverbs 16:9**: "In their hearts humans plan their course, but the Lord establishes their steps."
- **Isaiah 55:8-9**: "'For my thoughts are not your thoughts, neither are your ways my ways,' declares the Lord. 'As the heavens are higher than the earth, so are my ways higher than your ways and my thoughts than your thoughts.'"
- **Romans 8:28**: "And we know that in all things God works for the good of those who love him, who have been called according to his purpose."

Devotional Insight

Jeremiah 29:11 reminds us that God's plans are for our good, even when we face hardships. His plans include hope, a future, and blessings beyond what we can see.

Proverbs 16:9 teaches us that while we may make plans, it is ultimately God who directs our steps. Trusting His plan means being willing to adjust our course as He leads.

Isaiah 55:8-9 reminds us that God's ways are higher than ours. His perspective is infinite, and His plans are always rooted in His perfect wisdom and love.

Romans 8:28 assures us that God works all things—even the challenges and disappointments—for the good of those who love Him. Trusting His plan means believing that He can bring beauty from every situation.

Reflection Questions

1. Are there areas in your life where you're struggling to trust God's plan?
2. How can you surrender your own expectations and embrace His will?
3. When has God's plan proven better than your own, even if it didn't seem that way at first?

Practical Application

- **Surrender in Prayer**: Write down the areas where you're struggling to trust God and surrender them to Him in prayer.
- **Memorize His Promises**: Commit a verse like Jeremiah 29:11 or Romans 8:28 to memory, and remind yourself of it when doubt arises.
- **Seek His Direction**: Spend time in prayer and Scripture, asking God to guide your steps and give you peace as you follow His plan.

Closing Prayer

Lord,
Thank You for having a plan for our lives that is good, even when we don't understand it. Teach us to trust You in all circumstances and to surrender our desires to Your

will. Strengthen our faith and remind us that Your ways are higher than ours. Help us to rest in Your promises, knowing that You are always working for our good and Your glory. In Jesus' name, we pray. Amen.

Takeaway Thought

Trusting God's plan means believing in His wisdom, love, and faithfulness. Surrender your plans to Him, knowing that He is working all things for your good and His glory.

WALKING IN THE LIGHT OF GOD'S WORD

Opening Reflection

God's Word is a lamp for our feet and a light for our path, guiding us through the darkness of life's uncertainties. It provides wisdom, comfort, and truth, equipping us to make decisions that honor Him. Walking in the light of God's Word means allowing it to shape our actions, thoughts, and attitudes daily. Today, we'll explore how to let Scripture illuminate our path and lead us closer to God.

Opening Prayer

Father,
Thank You for the gift of Your Word, which is our source of truth and guidance. Teach us to cherish it, study it, and live by it every day. Help us to walk in its light and to trust

in the wisdom You've provided. Let Your Word transform our hearts and lead us into a deeper relationship with You. In Jesus' name, we pray. Amen.

Scripture Focus

- **Psalm 119:105**: "Your word is a lamp for my feet, a light on my path."
- **2 Timothy 3:16-17**: "All Scripture is God-breathed and is useful for teaching, rebuking, correcting, and training in righteousness, so that the servant of God may be thoroughly equipped for every good work."
- **Joshua 1:8**: "Keep this Book of the Law always on your lips; meditate on it day and night, so that you may be careful to do everything written in it. Then you will be prosperous and successful."
- **James 1:22**: "Do not merely listen to the word, and so deceive yourselves. Do what it says."

Devotional Insight

Psalm 119:105 reminds us that God's Word lights the way in moments of uncertainty. It gives clarity and direction when we don't know which step to take.

2 Timothy 3:16-17 teaches that Scripture equips us for every aspect of life. It corrects, encourages, and prepares us to live according to God's purpose.

Joshua 1:8 calls us to meditate on God's Word continually. By keeping it close to our hearts and applying it to our lives, we align ourselves with His will and experience His blessings.

James 1:22 challenges us to be doers of the Word, not just hearers. Walking in the light of God's Word means living out its teachings and allowing it to shape every area of our lives.

Reflection Questions

1. How often do you turn to God's Word for guidance and direction?
2. What steps can you take to meditate on Scripture more consistently?
3. Are there areas of your life where you've been hearing God's Word but struggling to act on it?

Practical Application

- **Daily Reading**: Set aside time each day to read and reflect on Scripture, asking God to reveal His truth to you.
- **Memorize Key Verses**: Choose a verse like Psalm 119:105 or Joshua 1:8 to memorize and carry with you throughout the day.
- **Live It Out**: Identify one area in your life where you can apply what you've learned from Scripture and take action this week.

Closing Prayer

Lord,
Thank You for the light of Your Word that guides us and strengthens us. Help us to be faithful in reading, meditating on, and applying it to our lives. Give us wisdom and clarity as we seek to walk in obedience to Your teachings. May Your Word be a lamp to our feet and a light for our path, drawing us closer to You each day. In Jesus' name, we pray. Amen.

Takeaway Thought

God's Word is a light that guides you, equips you, and transforms you. Walk in its truth daily, and let it illuminate the path God has prepared for you.

THE POWER OF UNITY IN CHRIST

Opening Reflection

Unity is a cornerstone of the Christian faith. Jesus prayed for His followers to be united so that the world would know the love of God. In a divided world, unity within the body of Christ is a powerful testimony of His grace and truth. Today, we'll explore how to foster unity in our relationships and communities, reflecting God's love and glorifying Him.

Opening Prayer

Lord,
Thank You for bringing us together as one body in Christ. Teach us to live in unity with one another, putting

aside our differences and focusing on Your love. Help us to be peacemakers, building bridges and strengthening relationships within the church and beyond. May our unity reflect Your glory and draw others to You. In Jesus' name, we pray. Amen.

Scripture Focus

- **John 17:21**: "That all of them may be one, Father, just as you are in me and I am in you. May they also be in us so that the world may believe that you have sent me."
- **Ephesians 4:3**: "Make every effort to keep the unity of the Spirit through the bond of peace."
- **Colossians 3:13-14**: "Bear with each other and forgive one another if any of you has a grievance against someone. Forgive as the Lord forgave you. And over all these virtues put on love, which binds them all together in perfect unity."
- **Psalm 133:1**: "How good and pleasant it is when God's people live together in unity!"

Devotional Insight

In John 17:21, Jesus prayed for the unity of all believers, emphasizing that our oneness reflects the love and truth of God to the world. Unity is not uniformity but a shared purpose in Christ.

Ephesians 4:3 challenges us to work toward unity by fostering peace within the body of Christ. Unity requires intentional effort and humility, empowered by the Holy Spirit.

Colossians 3:13-14 reminds us that love is the foundation of unity. Forgiveness and patience are essential for maintaining strong, healthy relationships that reflect Christ's character.

Psalm 133:1 highlights the beauty and blessing of unity among God's people. When we live in harmony, we experience God's joy and favor, and our lives become a testimony to His work in us.

Reflection Questions

1. Are there any divisions or unresolved conflicts in your relationships that need reconciliation?
2. How can you prioritize love and forgiveness to foster unity in your family, church, or community?
3. What steps can you take to contribute to the unity of the body of Christ?

Practical Application

- **Pray for Unity**: Regularly pray for unity in your church, family, and community, asking God to guide hearts toward reconciliation and peace.
- **Build Bridges**: Reach out to someone you may have had a conflict with and seek to restore the relationship through forgiveness and understanding.
- **Encourage Others**: Look for ways to build up and support others in the body of Christ, focusing on what unites rather than divides.

Closing Prayer

Lord,
Thank You for calling us to unity and giving us the example of perfect harmony through Your love. Help us to be peacemakers and bridge builders, reflecting Your grace in our relationships. Teach us to forgive, love, and support one another, putting Your kingdom above our

differences. May our unity bring glory to Your name and draw others to You. In Jesus' name, we pray. Amen.

Takeaway Thought

Unity in Christ is a powerful testimony to the world. Choose to prioritize love, forgiveness, and peace in your relationships, and let your life reflect the oneness we have in Him.

THE PROMISE OF GOD'S FAITHFULNESS

Opening Reflection

Life can be unpredictable, filled with ups and downs that test our faith. In these moments, we can cling to the truth that God is always faithful. His promises never fail, and His love remains constant through every season of life. Today, we'll reflect on the beauty of God's faithfulness and how it gives us confidence, strength, and hope.

Opening Prayer

Father,
Thank You for being a faithful God who never changes and never fails. Help us to trust in Your promises and to rest in the assurance of Your love. Strengthen our faith as we reflect on Your goodness, and remind us daily of

the many ways You've been faithful to us. May we walk in confidence, knowing that You are always with us. In Jesus' name, we pray. Amen.

Scripture Focus

- **Lamentations 3:22-23**: "Because of the Lord's great love we are not consumed, for his compassions never fail. They are new every morning; great is your faithfulness."
- **Deuteronomy 7:9**: "Know therefore that the Lord your God is God; he is the faithful God, keeping his covenant of love to a thousand generations of those who love him and keep his commandments."
- **2 Timothy 2:13**: "If we are faithless, he remains faithful, for he cannot disown himself."
- **Psalm 100:5**: "For the Lord is good and his love endures forever; his faithfulness continues through all generations."

Devotional Insight

Lamentations 3:22-23 reminds us that God's faithfulness is unchanging and renewed each day. His compassion and love sustain us, no matter what we face.

Deuteronomy 7:9 emphasizes God's covenant-keeping nature. His promises are trustworthy, and His faithfulness extends to all who follow Him.

2 Timothy 2:13 assures us that even when we falter in our faith, God remains faithful. His character is unchanging, and His love for us is constant.

Psalm 100:5 highlights the enduring nature of God's faithfulness. From generation to generation, His goodness and love remain the same, providing a firm foundation for our trust.

Reflection Questions

1. How has God shown His faithfulness to you in the past?
2. Are there promises of God you need to cling to in this season of your life?
3. How can you remind yourself of God's faithfulness when you face doubts or challenges?

Practical Application

- **Reflect on His Faithfulness**: Write down specific instances where God has shown His faithfulness in your life and thank Him for them.
- **Memorize a Verse**: Commit a verse like Lamentations 3:22-23 or Psalm 100:5 to memory and recite it when you need a reminder of God's promises.
- **Encourage Others**: Share a testimony of God's faithfulness with someone who may need encouragement to trust Him.

Closing Prayer

Lord,
Thank You for being a God who is always faithful. When life feels uncertain, help us to remember Your promises and trust in Your love. Strengthen our hearts and give us confidence in Your unchanging character. May we live in gratitude for all the ways You've been faithful and share

Your goodness with those around us. In Jesus' name, we pray. Amen.

Takeaway Thought

God's faithfulness is the anchor for our souls. Trust in His promises, reflect on His goodness, and walk confidently, knowing that He will never fail you.

EQUIPPED FOR THE BATTLE

Opening Reflection

As believers, we are engaged in a spiritual battle every day. The enemy seeks to distract, deceive, and destroy, but God has not left us defenseless. He has given us His armor and His Word to stand firm against every attack. Today, we'll explore how to recognize spiritual warfare, rely on God's power, and equip ourselves with the armor of God to live victoriously.

Opening Prayer

Father,
Thank You for being our defender and protector in the battles we face. Teach us to recognize the schemes of the

enemy and to rely on Your strength and wisdom. Equip us with Your armor so that we can stand firm in faith and walk in victory. May we trust in Your power to overcome every challenge. In Jesus' name, we pray. Amen.

Scripture Focus

- **Ephesians 6:11-13**: "Put on the full armor of God, so that you can take your stand against the devil's schemes. For our struggle is not against flesh and blood, but against the rulers, against the authorities, against the powers of this dark world and against the spiritual forces of evil in the heavenly realms. Therefore put on the full armor of God, so that when the day of evil comes, you may be able to stand your ground, and after you have done everything, to stand."
- **2 Corinthians 10:4-5**: "The weapons we fight with are not the weapons of the world. On the contrary, they have divine power to demolish strongholds. We demolish arguments and every pretension that sets itself up against the knowledge of God, and we take captive every thought to make it obedient to Christ."
- **James 4:7**: "Submit yourselves, then, to God. Resist the devil, and he will flee from you."
- **Romans 8:37**: "No, in all these things we are more than conquerors through him who loved us."

Devotional Insight

Ephesians 6:11-13 reminds us that our battle is spiritual, not physical. The enemy seeks to undermine our faith, but God has provided the armor we need to stand firm—truth, righteousness, peace, faith, salvation, and His Word.

In 2 Corinthians 10:4-5, we see that our weapons are spiritual, empowered by God to destroy strongholds. This means we can overcome lies, doubts, and fears by grounding ourselves in God's truth and taking every thought captive to obey Christ.

James 4:7 assures us that when we submit to God and resist the enemy, the devil will flee. Victory comes through reliance on God's power, not our own strength.

Romans 8:37 declares that we are more than conquerors through Christ. This victory is not conditional on our efforts but is secured through His love and sacrifice.

Reflection Questions

1. What battles are you currently facing in your life—spiritually, emotionally, or relationally?
2. Are you equipping yourself daily with the armor of God to stand firm against the enemy?
3. How can you rely on God's power, rather than your own, to walk in victory?

Practical Application

- **Put on the Armor Daily**: Read Ephesians 6:10-18 each morning, praying for God to clothe you with truth, righteousness, faith, and His Word as you face the day.
- **Identify the Enemy's Lies**: Write down any doubts or lies you're believing and counter them with specific promises from Scripture.
- **Resist Actively**: When temptations or spiritual attacks arise, stand firm by submitting to God in prayer and declaring His truth over your situation.

Closing Prayer

Lord,
Thank You for equipping us with Your armor and empowering us to stand firm in the face of spiritual battles. Help us to recognize the schemes of the enemy and to resist him with Your truth, faith, and righteousness. Strengthen us to trust in Your victory and to walk boldly as conquerors through Christ. May our lives reflect Your power and bring glory to Your name. In Jesus' name, we pray. Amen.

Takeaway Thought

God has provided everything you need to stand firm in spiritual battles. Put on His armor, rely on His strength, and walk in the victory that is already yours in Christ.

STRENGTH IN FELLOWSHIP

Opening Reflection

God designed us to live in community, not in isolation. Fellowship with other believers strengthens our faith, provides encouragement during difficult times, and allows us to grow together in Christ. Through unity and support, the body of Christ becomes a powerful force for God's kingdom. Today, we'll explore the importance of fellowship and how being connected with other believers helps us live out our faith.

Opening Prayer

Father,
Thank You for creating us to live in community with one another. Teach us to value fellowship and to encourage,

support, and build one another up in love. Help us to be active members of the body of Christ, working together to glorify You and to serve Your kingdom. In Jesus' name, we pray. Amen.

Scripture Focus

- **Hebrews 10:24-25**: "And let us consider how we may spur one another on toward love and good deeds, not giving up meeting together, as some are in the habit of doing, but encouraging one another—and all the more as you see the Day approaching."
- **Ecclesiastes 4:9-10**: "Two are better than one, because they have a good return for their labor: If either of them falls down, one can help the other up. But pity anyone who falls and has no one to help them up."
- **1 Thessalonians 5:11**: "Therefore encourage one another and build each other up, just as in fact you are doing."
- **Romans 12:4-5**: "For just as each of us has one body with many members, and these members do not all have the same function, so in Christ we, though many, form one body, and each member belongs to all the others."

Devotional Insight

Hebrews 10:24-25 reminds us to prioritize fellowship and to spur one another on in love and good deeds. Regularly gathering with other believers encourages us and strengthens our faith.

Ecclesiastes 4:9-10 emphasizes the strength found in partnership. When we face challenges, having others to support us and lift us up makes us stronger and more resilient.

1 Thessalonians 5:11 calls us to encourage and build each

other up. Fellowship provides a safe space to share burdens, celebrate victories, and grow together in faith.

Romans 12:4-5 illustrates the interconnectedness of the body of Christ. Each of us plays a unique role, and together we form a unified whole that reflects God's glory.

Reflection Questions

1. How has fellowship with other believers strengthened your faith?
2. Are there ways you can invest more intentionally in your church or community?
3. Who in your life might need encouragement or support, and how can you provide it?

Practical Application

- **Join a Small Group**: If you're not already in a small group or Bible study, find one where you can connect with others and grow in your faith together.
- **Encourage Someone**: This week, reach out to someone in your church or community who may need encouragement. Send them a note, call them, or spend time with them.
- **Participate Actively**: Find ways to serve in your church or community, using your gifts to build up the body of Christ and strengthen others.

Closing Prayer

Lord,
Thank You for the gift of fellowship and the encouragement that comes from being part of Your family. Help us to strengthen and support one another as we grow in faith and love. Teach us to value community and to be active participants in building Your kingdom together. May our relationships reflect Your grace and unity. In Jesus' name, we pray. Amen.

Takeaway Thought

Fellowship is a gift that strengthens your faith and equips you to support others. Stay connected to the body of Christ, encourage one another, and work together to glorify God.

WHO YOU ARE IN CHRIST

Opening Reflection

Our identity is often shaped by the world—our achievements, relationships, or failures. But as believers, our true identity is found in Christ. Knowing who you are in Him changes everything. It frees you from striving, anchors you in truth, and gives you confidence to live boldly for God's glory. Today, we'll explore what it means to embrace your identity in Christ and live as His beloved child.

Opening Prayer

Father,
Thank You for giving us a new identity in Christ. Help

us to see ourselves through Your eyes and to live in the freedom and confidence that comes from knowing who we are in You. Teach us to let go of the labels the world places on us and to rest in the truth of Your Word. May we reflect Your love and grace as Your children. In Jesus' name, we pray. Amen.

Scripture Focus

- **2 Corinthians 5:17**: "Therefore, if anyone is in Christ, the new creation has come: The old has gone, the new is here!"
- **Galatians 2:20**: "I have been crucified with Christ and I no longer live, but Christ lives in me. The life I now live in the body, I live by faith in the Son of God, who loved me and gave himself for me."
- **Ephesians 2:10**: "For we are God's handiwork, created in Christ Jesus to do good works, which God prepared in advance for us to do."
- **Romans 8:16-17**: "The Spirit himself testifies with our spirit that we are God's children. Now if we are children, then we are heirs—heirs of God and co-heirs with Christ, if indeed we share in his sufferings in order that we may also share in his glory."

Devotional Insight

2 Corinthians 5:17 reveals that being in Christ makes us a new creation. Our past no longer defines us because we have been transformed by His love and grace.

Galatians 2:20 reminds us that our lives are no longer our own. Christ lives in us, and we are empowered to live by faith in the One who gave His life for us.

Ephesians 2:10 declares that we are God's handiwork, uniquely designed and created for a purpose. Your identity in Christ means you are valuable and equipped to do the good works He has planned for you.

Romans 8:16-17 assures us that we are children of God and co-heirs with Christ. This identity gives us access to His promises, His love, and His eternal glory.

Reflection Questions

1. Are there labels or lies from the world that you've been believing about yourself? How can you replace them with God's truth?
2. How does knowing you are a new creation in Christ impact the way you view your past?
3. What steps can you take to live confidently in your identity as a child of God?

Practical Application

- **Speak Truth Over Yourself**: Write down a list of scriptures about your identity in Christ (e.g., 2 Corinthians 5:17, Ephesians 2:10). Read them daily to remind yourself of who you are.
- **Let Go of Labels**: Identify any negative labels you've been holding onto and replace them with the truth of God's Word.
- **Live Boldly**: Step out in faith this week, trusting that your identity in Christ equips you to fulfill His purposes for your life.

Closing Prayer

Lord,
Thank You for making us new creations in Christ. Help

us to walk confidently in the truth of who we are as Your children. Teach us to let go of the lies and labels that the world places on us and to embrace the identity You've given us. May our lives reflect Your love and grace as we live out the purpose You have for us. In Jesus' name, we pray. Amen.

Takeaway Thought

You are a new creation in Christ—loved, chosen, and equipped for a purpose. Embrace your identity as His child and live boldly in the freedom and confidence He provides.

WALKING IN OBEDIENCE

Opening Reflection

Obedience to God is an act of love, trust, and faith. It isn't always easy, and it often requires us to surrender our desires and follow His will instead. Yet, obedience brings us closer to God, aligns us with His purpose, and opens the door to blessings and spiritual growth. Today, we'll explore how to walk in obedience and experience the joy of living in alignment with God's Word.

Opening Prayer

Father,
Thank You for Your Word, which guides and teaches us.
Help us to trust You fully and to walk in obedience to Your

commands, even when it's difficult. Teach us to surrender our will to Yours and to live in a way that honors and glorifies You. Give us strength and courage to follow where You lead. In Jesus' name, we pray. Amen.

Scripture Focus

- **John 14:15**: "If you love me, keep my commands."
- **Deuteronomy 28:1-2**: "If you fully obey the Lord your God and carefully follow all his commands I give you today, the Lord your God will set you high above all the nations on earth. All these blessings will come on you and accompany you if you obey the Lord your God."
- **James 1:22**: "Do not merely listen to the word, and so deceive yourselves. Do what it says."
- **1 Samuel 15:22**: "But Samuel replied: 'Does the Lord delight in burnt offerings and sacrifices as much as in obeying the Lord? To obey is better than sacrifice, and to heed is better than the fat of rams.'"

Devotional Insight

John 14:15 teaches us that obedience is a natural expression of our love for Jesus. When we love Him, we trust His commands and follow them with joy.

Deuteronomy 28:1-2 reveals the blessings that come from obedience. God's promises are often tied to our willingness to follow Him fully and faithfully.

James 1:22 reminds us that true obedience goes beyond hearing God's Word—it requires action. Obedience is living out His truth in our daily lives.

1 Samuel 15:22 emphasizes that God desires our obedience more than outward acts of worship. True worship is reflected in

a heart that seeks to follow His will.

Reflection Questions

1. Are there areas of your life where you are struggling to obey God's commands?
2. How can you take practical steps to align your actions with God's Word?
3. What blessings or spiritual growth have you experienced through obedience in the past?

Practical Application

- **Examine Your Heart**: Reflect on areas where you may be resisting God's will. Pray for strength to surrender and trust Him fully.
- **Take One Step**: Identify one area where God is calling you to obedience and take a tangible step toward following His command this week.
- **Accountability**: Share your desire to walk in obedience with a trusted friend or mentor who can pray for you and encourage you.

Closing Prayer

Lord,
Thank You for calling us to live in obedience to You. Help us to trust Your Word and to follow Your commands with joy and faith. Teach us to surrender our desires and align our hearts with Your will. May our obedience bring glory

to Your name and draw us closer to You each day. In Jesus' name, we pray. Amen.

Takeaway Thought

Obedience is an act of love and trust that leads to spiritual growth and blessings. Follow God's Word faithfully, knowing that His plans for you are good and perfect.

THE VICTORY OF THE CROSS

Opening Reflection

The cross is the ultimate symbol of God's love and power. Through Jesus' sacrifice, we are set free from the bondage of sin, shame, and death. His resurrection is the victorious declaration that nothing can separate us from God's love. Today, we'll reflect on the significance of the cross and the resurrection, and how this victory shapes our daily lives as believers.

Opening Prayer

Father,
Thank You for the gift of the cross and the victory won through Jesus' sacrifice and resurrection. Help us to live in

the freedom and joy that come from knowing the power of Your love. Teach us to embrace the hope and victory of the cross every day and to share this truth with others. In Jesus' name, we pray. Amen.

Scripture Focus

- **1 Corinthians 15:55-57**: "Where, O death, is your victory? Where, O death, is your sting? The sting of death is sin, and the power of sin is the law. But thanks be to God! He gives us the victory through our Lord Jesus Christ."
- **Romans 5:8**: "But God demonstrates his own love for us in this: While we were still sinners, Christ died for us."
- **Colossians 2:13-15**: "When you were dead in your sins and in the uncircumcision of your flesh, God made you alive with Christ. He forgave us all our sins, having canceled the charge of our legal indebtedness, which stood against us and condemned us; he has taken it away, nailing it to the cross. And having disarmed the powers and authorities, he made a public spectacle of them, triumphing over them by the cross."
- **John 11:25-26**: "Jesus said to her, 'I am the resurrection and the life. The one who believes in me will live, even though they die; and whoever lives by believing in me will never die.'"

Devotional Insight

1 Corinthians 15:55-57 celebrates the victory of the cross, proclaiming that Jesus conquered death and sin once and for all. This victory is our source of hope and confidence.

Romans 5:8 reminds us of the depth of God's love. While we were still sinners, Jesus willingly gave His life for us, demonstrating the immeasurable grace of God.

Colossians 2:13-15 reveals that through the cross, God canceled the debt of our sin and defeated the powers of darkness. The cross is a public display of Christ's triumph and a reminder of our freedom.

John 11:25-26 offers the promise of eternal life through Jesus. His resurrection assures us that death has no hold on those who believe in Him.

Reflection Questions

1. How does the victory of the cross impact the way you live your daily life?
2. Are there areas where you struggle to fully embrace the freedom and forgiveness found in Jesus?
3. How can you share the message of the cross with someone in need of hope and redemption?

Practical Application

- **Reflect on the Cross**: Spend time in prayer or meditation, thanking Jesus for His sacrifice and reflecting on the freedom it brings.
- **Live in Freedom**: Identify any guilt, shame, or sin you're holding onto, and surrender it at the foot of the cross.
- **Share the Victory**: Share your testimony of how the cross has transformed your life with someone who needs encouragement or hope.

Closing Prayer

Lord,
Thank You for the victory of the cross and the gift of

salvation through Jesus. Help us to live boldly in the freedom and hope You have given us. Teach us to rely on Your power to overcome sin and to share the message of Your love with others. May the cross always be a reminder of Your grace and victory in our lives. In Jesus' name, we pray. Amen.

Takeaway Thought

The cross is a symbol of victory, love, and freedom. Embrace its power in your life, live in the hope of the resurrection, and share the good news of Christ's triumph with the world.

LIVING WITH ETERNAL PERSPECTIVE

Opening Reflection

It's easy to get caught up in the demands and worries of daily life. But as believers, we're called to live with an eternal perspective, focusing on what truly matters in light of eternity. When we fix our eyes on what is unseen, we find hope, purpose, and motivation to live for God's glory. Today, we'll explore how to align our hearts and actions with eternity in mind.

Opening Prayer

Lord,
Thank You for the promise of eternal life with You. Teach us to live each day with an eternal perspective, focusing on the things that matter most to You. Help us to let go of temporary distractions and to invest in what has lasting value. Strengthen our hearts with the hope of eternity

and guide us to live for Your glory. In Jesus' name, we pray. Amen.

Scripture Focus

- **Colossians 3:2**: "Set your minds on things above, not on earthly things."
- **2 Corinthians 4:17-18**: "For our light and momentary troubles are achieving for us an eternal glory that far outweighs them all. So we fix our eyes not on what is seen, but on what is unseen, since what is seen is temporary, but what is unseen is eternal."
- **Matthew 6:19-21**: "Do not store up for yourselves treasures on earth, where moths and vermin destroy, and where thieves break in and steal. But store up for yourselves treasures in heaven, where moths and vermin do not destroy, and where thieves do not break in and steal. For where your treasure is, there your heart will be also."
- **Philippians 3:20**: "But our citizenship is in heaven. And we eagerly await a Savior from there, the Lord Jesus Christ."

Devotional Insight

Colossians 3:2 reminds us to shift our focus from temporary, earthly concerns to the eternal realities of heaven. This perspective helps us prioritize God's kingdom above all else.

In 2 Corinthians 4:17-18, Paul encourages us to view our trials in light of eternity. Even our struggles have purpose, preparing us for the eternal glory that far outweighs the challenges we face.

Matthew 6:19-21 calls us to invest in eternal treasures. By focusing on God's purposes and serving others, we store up treasures in heaven that will never fade.

Philippians 3:20 reminds us that our true home is in heaven. Living with an eternal perspective means embracing our identity as citizens of God's kingdom and living in anticipation of Christ's return.

Reflection Questions

1. Are there areas of your life where you've been overly focused on temporary concerns?
2. How can living with an eternal perspective give you hope and clarity in challenging situations?
3. What steps can you take to store up treasures in heaven and focus on what matters most?

Practical Application

- **Prioritize Eternal Investments**: Identify one area where you can invest in God's kingdom—serving others, giving generously, or sharing the gospel.
- **Let Go of Distractions**: Evaluate your daily priorities and remove things that keep you overly focused on temporary concerns.
- **Encourage Others**: Share the hope of eternity with someone who may be feeling discouraged or overwhelmed.

Closing Prayer

Lord,
Thank You for the hope and promise of eternity with You. Help us to live each day with an eternal perspective, trusting that our trials are preparing us for eternal glory. Teach us to focus on what truly matters and to invest in treasures that last forever. May our lives reflect the hope and joy of Your kingdom, drawing others closer to You. In Jesus' name, we pray. Amen.

Takeaway Thought

Living with an eternal perspective transforms how you face trials, set priorities, and invest your time and energy. Fix your eyes on what is unseen, and live for God's glory in light of eternity.

FREE FROM CONDEMNATION

Opening Reflection

Guilt and shame can weigh us down, making us feel unworthy of God's love. But through Jesus, we are set free from condemnation. His sacrifice on the cross removes our sin and allows us to walk in freedom and grace. Today, we'll explore how to live free from guilt and shame by embracing God's forgiveness and the truth of our identity in Christ.

Opening Prayer

Father,
Thank You for the freedom we have in Christ. Help us to let go of guilt and shame, knowing that we are

forgiven and no longer condemned. Teach us to walk in the fullness of Your grace, living boldly as Your redeemed children. May we trust in Your promises and embrace the freedom You've given us. In Jesus' name, we pray. Amen.

Scripture Focus

- **Romans 8:1**: "Therefore, there is now no condemnation for those who are in Christ Jesus."
- **Isaiah 1:18**: "'Come now, let us settle the matter,' says the Lord. 'Though your sins are like scarlet, they shall be as white as snow; though they are red as crimson, they shall be like wool.'"
- **Psalm 103:12**: "As far as the east is from the west, so far has he removed our transgressions from us."
- **1 John 1:9**: "If we confess our sins, he is faithful and just and will forgive us our sins and purify us from all unrighteousness."

Devotional Insight

Romans 8:1 is a powerful reminder that in Christ, we are no longer under condemnation. His sacrifice removes the penalty of sin, allowing us to live in freedom and peace.

Isaiah 1:18 illustrates God's willingness to cleanse us completely, no matter how deep or visible our sins may seem. His grace makes us new, removing every stain of sin.

Psalm 103:12 reassures us that God has removed our sins entirely. When we repent, He forgives us and no longer holds our past against us.

1 John 1:9 reminds us of God's faithfulness in forgiving our sins. When we confess, He purifies us, removing guilt and shame

and restoring us to a right relationship with Him.

Reflection Questions

1. Are there past mistakes or sins you struggle to forgive yourself for? How can you surrender them to God?
2. How does the truth of Romans 8:1—no condemnation in Christ—impact the way you view yourself?
3. Who in your life could benefit from hearing the message of God's forgiveness and grace?

Practical Application

- **Release Guilt**: Write down any sins or feelings of guilt that weigh you down. Pray over them, asking God for forgiveness, and then destroy the list as a symbolic act of letting them go.
- **Memorize Romans 8:1**: Repeat this verse daily to remind yourself that you are free from condemnation in Christ.
- **Encourage Someone**: Share the truth of God's forgiveness with a friend or loved one who may be struggling with guilt or shame.

Closing Prayer

Lord,
Thank You for setting us free from condemnation through Christ's sacrifice. Help us to walk in the freedom of Your grace, letting go of guilt and shame. Teach us to trust in Your forgiveness and to see ourselves as You see us—redeemed, loved, and set free. May we share this hope with others and live boldly for Your glory. In Jesus' name, we pray. Amen.

Takeaway Thought

In Christ, you are no longer condemned. Let go of guilt and shame, and live in the freedom of God's forgiveness and grace. You are His beloved and redeemed child.

FAITHFUL WITH WHAT YOU HAVE

Opening Reflection

God entrusts each of us with time, talents, and resources, calling us to use them for His glory. Being faithful with what we have, no matter how small it seems, reflects our trust in Him as the ultimate Provider. Today, we'll explore how to live as faithful stewards, honoring God with everything He's given us.

Opening Prayer

Lord,
Thank You for entrusting us with time, talents, and resources to use for Your kingdom. Teach us to be faithful

stewards of what You've given, using all that we have to bring glory to Your name. Help us to trust You as our Provider and to give with hearts full of joy and gratitude. In Jesus' name, we pray. Amen.

Scripture Focus

- **Matthew 25:21**: "His master replied, 'Well done, good and faithful servant! You have been faithful with a few things; I will put you in charge of many things. Come and share your master's happiness!'"
- **Colossians 3:23-24**: "Whatever you do, work at it with all your heart, as working for the Lord, not for human masters, since you know that you will receive an inheritance from the Lord as a reward. It is the Lord Christ you are serving."
- **Proverbs 3:9-10**: "Honor the Lord with your wealth, with the firstfruits of all your crops; then your barns will be filled to overflowing, and your vats will brim over with new wine."
- **1 Peter 4:10**: "Each of you should use whatever gift you have received to serve others, as faithful stewards of God's grace in its various forms."

Devotional Insight

Matthew 25:21 shows us that faithfulness in small things leads to greater opportunities in God's kingdom. When we steward well what we've been given, we bring joy to the Lord.

Colossians 3:23-24 reminds us that everything we do should be done for God's glory. Whether in work, relationships, or ministry, our efforts become an act of worship when done wholeheartedly for Him.

Proverbs 3:9-10 emphasizes honoring God with our resources,

giving Him the first and best of what we have. Trusting Him as our Provider allows us to give generously and joyfully.

1 Peter 4:10 calls us to use our unique gifts to serve others, recognizing that everything we have is a gift from God meant to bless those around us.

Reflection Questions

1. Are there areas of your life where you could be more faithful with what God has entrusted to you?
2. How can you use your time, talents, or resources to serve others and glorify God?
3. Do you trust God as your ultimate Provider, or are you holding back in any area of giving or serving?

Practical Application

- **Assess Your Stewardship**: Reflect on how you're using your time, talents, and resources. Identify one area where you can be more intentional in honoring God.
- **Give Generously**: This week, give your time, money, or abilities to bless someone in need, trusting God to provide as you give.
- **Serve with Joy**: Use a specific gift or talent you have to serve your church or community, offering it as worship to God.

Closing Prayer

Lord,
Thank You for every good gift You have placed in our lives. Help us to be faithful stewards of all You've given, using our time, talents, and resources to honor You and bless others. Teach us to trust in Your provision and to

give with joyful hearts. May our faithfulness bring glory to Your name and inspire others to seek You. In Jesus' name, we pray. Amen.

Takeaway Thought

Being faithful with what you have honors God and opens the door for greater opportunities to serve Him. Trust in His provision, and use your gifts to bless others and glorify His name.

THE GOD WHO NEVER CHANGES

Opening Reflection

Life is full of changes—seasons shift, circumstances evolve, and people come and go. But in the midst of uncertainty, we can find comfort in the unchanging nature of God. His love, promises, and faithfulness remain constant through every moment of our lives. Today, we'll explore how God's immutability gives us peace and confidence, no matter what life brings.

Opening Prayer

Father,
Thank You for being a God who never changes. In a world

full of uncertainty, we find peace in Your constant love and faithfulness. Teach us to trust in Your unchanging promises and to anchor our hearts in the truth of who You are. Help us to rest in Your steadfast presence today and always. In Jesus' name, we pray. Amen.

Scripture Focus

- **Hebrews 13:8**: "Jesus Christ is the same yesterday and today and forever."
- **Malachi 3:6**: "I the Lord do not change. So you, the descendants of Jacob, are not destroyed."
- **James 1:17**: "Every good and perfect gift is from above, coming down from the Father of the heavenly lights, who does not change like shifting shadows."
- **Psalm 102:25-27**: "In the beginning you laid the foundations of the earth, and the heavens are the work of your hands. They will perish, but you remain; they will all wear out like a garment. Like clothing you will change them and they will be discarded. But you remain the same, and your years will never end."

Devotional Insight

Hebrews 13:8 declares the unchanging nature of Christ. His character, love, and promises remain constant, giving us a firm foundation for our faith.

Malachi 3:6 reassures us that God's unchanging nature is the reason we are secure. His faithfulness ensures that His plans for us will always prevail.

James 1:17 highlights God as the giver of every good and perfect gift. Unlike the shifting circumstances of life, God's goodness is constant and dependable.

Psalm 102:25-27 reminds us that while the world around us changes and fades, God remains eternal and unchanging. His constancy provides peace and security in an ever-changing world.

Reflection Questions

1. How does knowing that God never changes bring you peace in uncertain times?
2. Are there promises in God's Word that you can hold onto as reminders of His unchanging nature?
3. How can you reflect God's consistency and faithfulness in your relationships and actions?

Practical Application

- **Anchor in God's Promises**: Identify a specific promise from Scripture that speaks to God's unchanging nature and meditate on it this week.
- **Reflect on God's Faithfulness**: Write down examples of how God's consistency has been evident in your life during times of change.
- **Share God's Steadfastness**: Encourage someone going through a season of uncertainty by sharing how God's unchanging nature has brought you peace.

Closing Prayer

Lord,
Thank You for being our unchanging God, the One we can depend on in every season of life. Teach us to trust in Your steadfast love and faithfulness, even when everything

around us feels uncertain. Help us to rest in the peace that comes from knowing You are the same yesterday, today, and forever. May Your unchanging nature give us confidence to walk in faith and share Your love with others. In Jesus' name, we pray. Amen.

Takeaway Thought

In a world of constant change, God remains the same. Trust in His unchanging nature, rely on His promises, and find peace in the consistency of His love and faithfulness.

FINDING JOY IN HARDSHIPS

Opening Reflection

Hardships are an inevitable part of life, but they don't have to rob us of joy. The Bible teaches us that even in trials, we can find a deep and abiding joy when we trust in God's purposes. Hardships are often the very tools God uses to grow our faith, refine our character, and draw us closer to Him. Today, we'll explore how to find joy in the midst of difficulty by focusing on God's goodness and faithfulness.

Opening Prayer

Father,
Thank You for being with us in every season, especially in times of hardship. Teach us to see our trials through the

lens of Your purpose and to find joy in the work You're doing in us. Help us to trust in Your plans and to hold onto the hope that comes from knowing You. May Your joy be our strength. In Jesus' name, we pray. Amen.

Scripture Focus

- **James 1:2-3**: "Consider it pure joy, my brothers and sisters, whenever you face trials of many kinds, because you know that the testing of your faith produces perseverance."
- **Romans 5:3-4**: "Not only so, but we also glory in our sufferings, because we know that suffering produces perseverance; perseverance, character; and character, hope."
- **1 Peter 1:6-7**: "In all this you greatly rejoice, though now for a little while you may have had to suffer grief in all kinds of trials. These have come so that the proven genuineness of your faith—of greater worth than gold, which perishes even though refined by fire—may result in praise, glory and honor when Jesus Christ is revealed."
- **Nehemiah 8:10**: "Do not grieve, for the joy of the Lord is your strength."

Devotional Insight

James 1:2-3 challenges us to see trials as opportunities for growth. Though trials are difficult, they produce perseverance, strengthening our faith for the journey ahead.

Romans 5:3-4 reminds us that suffering has a purpose. It refines our character and builds hope, anchoring us in God's promises.

1 Peter 1:6-7 highlights that trials refine our faith, making it more valuable than gold. When we endure hardships with joy,

we bring glory to God and grow closer to Him.

Nehemiah 8:10 teaches us that God's joy is our source of strength. Even in the midst of difficulty, we can find joy by resting in His presence and trusting in His power.

Reflection Questions

1. What challenges are you currently facing, and how can you invite God's joy into those circumstances?
2. How has God used past hardships to grow your faith or shape your character?
3. What practical steps can you take to focus on God's goodness and promises during difficult times?

Practical Application

- **Keep a Gratitude Journal**: Write down three things you're thankful for each day, even in the midst of trials, to remind yourself of God's faithfulness.
- **Pray Through Trials**: Bring your hardships to God in prayer, asking Him to help you see His purposes and to give you strength and joy.
- **Encourage Someone Else**: Share your story of how God has worked in your life through trials, and encourage someone who may be going through a similar hardship.

Closing Prayer

Lord,
Thank You for the joy that comes from knowing You and trusting in Your purposes. Help us to find joy in the midst of trials, knowing that You are using them to refine us and draw us closer to You. Strengthen our hearts and fill

us with hope as we rest in Your goodness. May our faith shine brightly, even in difficult times, bringing glory to Your name. In Jesus' name, we pray. Amen.

Takeaway Thought

Hardships are opportunities for growth and deeper trust in God. Embrace the joy that comes from His presence and His promise to work all things for your good and His glory.

THE POWER OF GOD'S GRACE

Opening Reflection

God's grace is one of the most transformative gifts we receive as believers. It's unearned, undeserved, and abundant, covering our weaknesses and empowering us to live for Him. Grace is not only the foundation of our salvation but also the strength that sustains us daily. Today, we'll explore how to fully embrace God's grace and allow it to transform our lives.

Opening Prayer

Father,
Thank You for Your amazing grace that saves, sustains, and strengthens us. Teach us to live in the fullness of Your

grace, letting go of guilt and striving. Help us to trust in Your sufficiency and to reflect Your grace in how we treat others. May Your grace empower us to walk in faith and obedience each day. In Jesus' name, we pray. Amen.

Scripture Focus

- **Ephesians 2:8-9**: "For it is by grace you have been saved, through faith—and this is not from yourselves, it is the gift of God—not by works, so that no one can boast."
- **2 Corinthians 12:9**: "But he said to me, 'My grace is sufficient for you, for my power is made perfect in weakness.' Therefore I will boast all the more gladly about my weaknesses, so that Christ's power may rest on me."
- **Romans 6:14**: "For sin shall no longer be your master, because you are not under the law, but under grace."
- **Hebrews 4:16**: "Let us then approach God's throne of grace with confidence, so that we may receive mercy and find grace to help us in our time of need."

Devotional Insight

Ephesians 2:8-9 reminds us that grace is a gift. We cannot earn it through works; it is freely given by God because of His great love for us.

2 Corinthians 12:9 shows us that God's grace is sufficient for every weakness. Instead of hiding our struggles, we can rely on His grace to give us strength.

Romans 6:14 declares that we are no longer slaves to sin because of God's grace. It empowers us to live in freedom and victory.

Hebrews 4:16 invites us to approach God's throne of grace

boldly. We can confidently seek His help, knowing that His grace is available to meet every need.

Reflection Questions

1. Are there areas in your life where you've been trying to earn God's favor instead of relying on His grace?
2. How does knowing God's grace is sufficient for your weaknesses change the way you view yourself and your challenges?
3. How can you extend God's grace to someone else this week?

Practical Application

- **Accept His Grace**: Spend time in prayer, surrendering any feelings of guilt, shame, or striving, and rest in God's unearned favor.
- **Reflect His Grace**: Look for opportunities to show grace to others, especially in situations where it's difficult.
- **Rely on His Strength**: In moments of weakness or challenge, remind yourself of 2 Corinthians 12:9 and ask God for the strength His grace provides.

Closing Prayer

Lord,
Thank You for the gift of Your grace that saves us and sustains us each day. Help us to trust in Your sufficiency, letting go of striving and resting in Your love. Teach us to reflect Your grace in how we treat others, showing compassion, forgiveness, and patience. May Your grace empower us to live boldly for You and bring glory to Your

name. In Jesus' name, we pray. Amen.

Takeaway Thought

God's grace is a gift that saves, strengthens, and sustains you. Embrace it fully, rest in its sufficiency, and let it empower you to live for His glory.

TRUSTING GOD IN UNCERTAIN TIMES

Opening Reflection

The world today is filled with uncertainty—economic challenges, political tensions, health crises, and natural disasters. It's easy to feel overwhelmed or anxious, but God calls us to trust Him even in the most chaotic seasons. When we anchor our faith in Him, we find peace and hope that transcend the instability around us. Today, we'll explore how to trust God when everything seems uncertain.

Opening Prayer

Lord,
Thank You for being our rock and refuge in times of uncertainty. Help us to fix our eyes on You, trusting in

Your plans and promises. Teach us to release our fears and anxieties, knowing that You are in control. Fill us with peace and hope as we navigate the challenges of the world today. In Jesus' name, we pray. Amen.

Scripture Focus

- **Isaiah 41:10**: "So do not fear, for I am with you; do not be dismayed, for I am your God. I will strengthen you and help you; I will uphold you with my righteous right hand."
- **John 14:27**: "Peace I leave with you; my peace I give you. I do not give to you as the world gives. Do not let your hearts be troubled and do not be afraid."
- **Psalm 46:1-2**: "God is our refuge and strength, an ever-present help in trouble. Therefore we will not fear, though the earth give way and the mountains fall into the heart of the sea."
- **Matthew 6:34**: "Therefore do not worry about tomorrow, for tomorrow will worry about itself. Each day has enough trouble of its own."

Devotional Insight

Isaiah 41:10 reminds us that God's presence and strength are constant. Even when the world feels unstable, He upholds us with His righteous hand.

In John 14:27, Jesus offers us His peace—a peace that the world cannot give. This peace is rooted in His sovereignty and love, not in external circumstances.

Psalm 46:1-2 declares that God is our refuge and strength, even when everything around us seems to collapse. We can rest in His unshakable stability.

Matthew 6:34 encourages us to focus on today, trusting that

God will provide for tomorrow. Worry adds nothing to our lives, but faith in God sustains us.

Reflection Questions

1. What current events or uncertainties are causing you anxiety or fear?
2. How can you shift your focus from the chaos of the world to the promises of God?
3. How can you be a source of peace and encouragement to those struggling with fear and uncertainty?

Practical Application

- **Limit Negative Input**: Reduce time spent dwelling on distressing news and instead spend more time in prayer and God's Word.
- **Anchor in God's Promises**: Choose a verse like Isaiah 41:10 or Psalm 46:1 to meditate on when you feel overwhelmed by current events.
- **Encourage Others**: Share God's peace with someone who is struggling with fear or anxiety, offering to pray with them or share uplifting scripture.

Closing Prayer

Lord,
Thank You for being our refuge in uncertain times. Teach us to rely on Your strength and to trust in Your promises when the world feels unstable. Help us to be lights of hope and peace to those around us, pointing them to the

security found in You. May our faith in You bring calm to the storms we face. In Jesus' name, we pray. Amen.

Takeaway Thought

God remains in control, even when the world feels chaotic. Trust in His presence, rely on His promises, and let His peace carry you through every uncertainty.

BEING A LIGHT IN A DIVIDED WORLD

Opening Reflection

Our world today is deeply divided—politically, socially, and culturally. These divisions can create conflict, misunderstanding, and a sense of hopelessness. As followers of Christ, we are called to be peacemakers and a light in the darkness. By living out God's love and truth, we can bring healing and unity to a fractured world. Today, we'll reflect on how to be a light in the midst of division.

Opening Prayer

Lord,
Thank You for calling us to be Your light in a world

that desperately needs healing. Help us to reflect Your love, grace, and truth in every interaction. Teach us to be peacemakers and bridge builders, showing the world what it means to follow You. May our lives bring unity and hope in the midst of division. In Jesus' name, we pray. Amen.

Scripture Focus

- **Matthew 5:14-16**: "You are the light of the world. A town built on a hill cannot be hidden. Neither do people light a lamp and put it under a bowl. Instead, they put it on its stand, and it gives light to everyone in the house. In the same way, let your light shine before others, that they may see your good deeds and glorify your Father in heaven."
- **Romans 12:18**: "If it is possible, as far as it depends on you, live at peace with everyone."
- **Colossians 4:6**: "Let your conversation be always full of grace, seasoned with salt, so that you may know how to answer everyone."
- **Galatians 3:28**: "There is neither Jew nor Gentile, neither slave nor free, nor is there male and female, for you are all one in Christ Jesus."

Devotional Insight

Matthew 5:14-16 reminds us that we are called to shine God's light in a world filled with darkness. Our lives should point others to His love and truth.

Romans 12:18 encourages us to pursue peace as far as it depends on us. Even in the face of disagreement, we can choose grace and understanding.

Colossians 4:6 teaches us to speak with kindness and wisdom.

Our words should build bridges, not walls, and reflect the love of Christ.

Galatians 3:28 emphasizes unity in Christ. Despite our differences, we are all equal in His eyes, and this truth should guide how we treat one another.

Reflection Questions

1. How can you be a light in the midst of the divisions in your community or world?
2. Are there ways you can bring peace and understanding to a relationship or situation filled with conflict?
3. How can your actions and words reflect God's love and truth in a divided world?

Practical Application

- **Be a Peacemaker**: Reach out to someone with whom you have a disagreement or misunderstanding, seeking to build understanding and unity.
- **Reflect God's Love**: Perform an act of kindness this week for someone with differing views or beliefs as a way to reflect Christ's love.
- **Pray for Unity**: Spend time praying for unity in your family, church, community, and the world, asking God to heal divisions.

Closing Prayer

Lord,
Thank You for calling us to be Your light in a divided world. Help us to bring peace, love, and understanding to those around us. Teach us to reflect Your grace in every conversation and action, and to be bridge builders who

point others to You. May our lives shine brightly, drawing people to Your truth and healing. In Jesus' name, we pray. Amen.

Takeaway Thought

In a divided world, you are called to be a light. Reflect God's love, pursue peace, and live in a way that points others to His healing and truth.

STARTING FRESH: A JOURNEY WITH CHRIST

Opening Reflection

Becoming a follower of Christ is the beginning of an incredible journey. It's not about being perfect but about walking with Jesus, learning from Him, and growing in faith. As a new believer, you are now part of God's family, and He will guide you every step of the way. Today, we'll explore the foundational truths to help you start strong in your relationship with Christ.

Opening Prayer

Father,
Thank You for the gift of salvation and the new life You've given us in Christ. Help us to grow in our faith, to trust You in every step, and to seek You daily. Teach us

to walk in Your ways and to rely on Your strength as we begin this journey with You. May we always find joy and peace in Your presence. In Jesus' name, we pray. Amen.

Scripture Focus

- **2 Corinthians 5:17**: "Therefore, if anyone is in Christ, the new creation has come: The old has gone, the new is here!"
- **John 15:5**: "I am the vine; you are the branches. If you remain in me and I in you, you will bear much fruit; apart from me you can do nothing."
- **Psalm 119:105**: "Your word is a lamp for my feet, a light on my path."
- **Matthew 28:19-20**: "Therefore go and make disciples of all nations, baptizing them in the name of the Father and of the Son and of the Holy Spirit, and teaching them to obey everything I have commanded you. And surely I am with you always, to the very end of the age."

Devotional Insight

2 Corinthians 5:17 assures us that in Christ, we are made new. Your past no longer defines you—God has given you a fresh start.

John 15:5 highlights the importance of staying connected to Jesus. By remaining in Him through prayer, worship, and studying His Word, you will grow and bear spiritual fruit.

Psalm 119:105 reminds us that God's Word is our guide. Reading the Bible regularly will help you understand His will and navigate life's challenges.

Matthew 28:19-20 is a call to share your faith with others. As a new believer, you are part of God's mission to bring His love and truth to the world, knowing that He is always with you.

Reflection Questions

1. What excites you most about beginning your journey with Christ?
2. What steps can you take to grow closer to Jesus each day?
3. How can you share your new faith with others, even in small ways?

Practical Application

- **Start with the Bible**: Begin reading the Gospel of John to learn more about who Jesus is and what He taught.
- **Pray Daily**: Spend time each day talking to God, thanking Him, and asking for His guidance.
- **Join a Church or Group**: Connect with other believers who can encourage you, answer your questions, and walk alongside you in your faith journey.

Closing Prayer

Lord,
Thank You for this new life in Christ. Help us to grow in faith and to trust You in every part of our journey. Teach us to rely on Your Word, stay connected to You, and share Your love with others. Guide us as we take our first steps, and remind us daily that You are always with us. May our lives reflect Your glory and bring honor to Your name. In Jesus' name, we pray. Amen.

Takeaway Thought

As a new believer, you are a new creation in Christ. Stay connected to Him, grow in His Word, and trust Him to guide you every step of the way on this exciting journey of faith.

EPILOGUE: A LIFE TRANSFORMED BY GOD

As you close this devotional, take a moment to reflect on the journey you've walked through its pages. From exploring God's promises to trusting His plan, from embracing His grace to living with purpose, each chapter has been a step toward a deeper relationship with the Creator who loves you more than you can imagine.

The truths you've read are not just for a season—they are the foundation for a lifetime of faith. The journey of knowing God and growing in Christ is lifelong, full of discovery, transformation, and hope. There will be challenges, but remember that you are never walking alone. God is with you, guiding, strengthening, and equipping you every step of the way.

Your life is a testimony to His love and faithfulness. As you live out what you've learned, allow God to work through you to impact the world around you. You are part of His story, uniquely created to glorify Him and to bring His light to others.

A Few Final Encouragements

1. **Stay Rooted in God's Word**: Let the Bible be your guide and source of strength. Continue to meditate on Scripture and apply it to your daily life.
2. **Pray Without Ceasing**: Make prayer a daily conversation with God. Bring Him your joys, your struggles, and your dreams.
3. **Live in Community**: Surround yourself with fellow believers who will encourage and challenge you to grow in your faith.
4. **Walk in Obedience**: Trust God's plans for your life and follow His lead. Remember that obedience brings blessings and draws you closer to Him.
5. **Shine His Light**: Share the love, grace, and truth of Christ with others. Your story can inspire and encourage someone to take their first steps of faith.

A Closing Prayer

Father,
Thank You for the journey we've walked together through this devotional. Thank You for the truths You've revealed, the growth You've inspired, and the hope You've given us. Help us to live out what we've learned and to walk boldly in faith, trusting You in every moment. Strengthen our hearts, guide our steps, and use our lives for Your glory.

May we shine Your light in a world that needs You. In Jesus' name, we pray. Amen.

Takeaway Thought

Your journey with God doesn't end here—it's just beginning. Stay close to Him, grow in His Word, and trust Him to lead you into the abundant life He has planned. A life transformed by God is a life that reflects His glory and makes an eternal impact.

DAILY/WEEKLY PLANNER PAGE LAYOUT

REFLECTION & JOURNALING

Date: _____

- **What spoke to you most from this chapter?**
  Write down key takeaways or insights from today's reading.

  _____

- **What Scripture stood out to you today?**
  Note any verses that particularly resonated with you.

  _____

- **How do you feel God is speaking to you through this chapter?**
  Reflect on any personal messages, challenges, or encouragements.

  _____

- **Prayer:**
  Take a moment to pray. Here's a prompt if you need one:
  "God, help me to apply what I've learned today, and guide me as I walk in faith and trust You more fully."

  _____

Weekly Goal Setting

Week of: _____

1. **How will I apply what I've learned this week?**

Reflect on practical ways to incorporate the lessons into your daily life.

---

2. **What steps will I take this week to deepen my relationship with God?**
   Consider specific actions, like daily prayer, Bible reading, or acts of kindness.

---

3. **Who can I encourage or share this truth with?**
   Think of someone in your life who could benefit from the lessons you've learned.

---

4. **What is one area of my life where I need to trust God more fully?**
   Consider a challenge or struggle that requires deeper faith.

Answered Prayers & Reflection
Answered Prayers this Week:

- **Prayer 1:** *Describe a prayer request you brought to God.*

- **Prayer 2:** *What has God revealed to you through answered prayer?*

- **Prayer 3:** *Have you seen God's faithfulness in action? How did He respond?*

Weekly Gratitude & Reflections

- **Three things I'm thankful for this week:**

- **One way I saw God working in my life this week:**
  Share a testimony or moment where you saw God's hand moving.

- **One thing I will surrender to God this week:**
  Reflect on areas of struggle or doubt you need to release to Him.

Additional Features for Personal Growth:

- **Scripture Memorization Section:**
  Write out a verse you want to commit to memory this week.

- **Thoughts & Reflections:**
  Leave space for additional notes, thoughts, or personal revelations.

How to Use This Page:

1. **Daily Reflections**: Fill in the **Journaling** section after each chapter to process what you're learning and how God is speaking to you.
2. **Weekly Goals**: At the start of each week, take time to set goals and reflect on how you can live out the truth of that week's chapters.
3. **Answered Prayers**: Track your prayers and God's responses throughout the week to build confidence in His faithfulness.
4. **Gratitude and Surrender**: This section helps you focus

on God's blessings and areas where you need to trust Him more deeply.

HYMN: MORE THAN CONQUERORS

(Inspired by Romans 8:37, 2 Corinthians 12:9, and Ephesians 6:10-11)

Verse 1:
Through valleys low and peaks so high,
By faith alone, on Christ rely.
His Word our sword, His truth our shield,
In Him, our victory is sealed.

Chorus:
By His grace, we stand secure,
In Christ alone, we shall endure.
With Christ's strength, we shall not fall,
For God is sovereign over all.
More than conquerors in His might,
Led by His love, we walk in light.

Verse 2:
Though storms may rage and darkness rise,
Our hope is fixed beyond the skies.
His peace sustains, His hands uphold,
His mercy writes our story bold.

Chorus:
By His grace, we stand secure,
In Christ alone, we shall endure.
With Christ's strength, we shall not fall,

For God is sovereign over all.
More than conquerors in His might,
Led by His love, we walk in light.

Verse 3:
The chains of sin are torn apart,
By Christ's own blood, a brand-new heart.
His Spirit leads, His power stays,
We walk in faith all of our days.

Chorus:
By His grace, we stand secure,
In Christ alone, we shall endure.
With Christ's strength, we shall not fall,
For God is sovereign over all.
More than conquerors in His might,
Led by His love, we walk in light.

Bridge:
With lifted hands, we praise His name,
For in His love, we stand unshamed.
The grave is crushed, the battle won,
Through Christ, the risen, glorious One!

Chorus (Final):
By His grace, we stand secure,
In Christ alone, we shall endure.
With Christ's strength, we shall not fall,
For God is sovereign over all.
More than conquerors in His might,
Led by His love, we walk in light.

www.ingramcontent.com/pod-product-compliance
Lightning Source LLC
Chambersburg PA
CBHW060149050426
42446CB00013B/2735

APPENDIX C

9	Rapture (happiness/bliss)	Delight or joyful interest in an object of examination	Pervading the mind-body with ecstasy	• Exultation of consciousness • Elation • Uplifting or lightness of the body	Rapture, happiness, bliss
10	Concentration	• Non-distraction • One-pointedness of mind	• Unifying all mental phenomena • Contemplating on an object • Meditating on an object	• Peacefulness of consciousness • Mental absorption	
11	Resolution	• Conviction and fervor • Sincerity	• Confirming, • Non-groping	• Determination • Unshakability • Decision	Being certain or convinced about something
12	Vigor	• Energetic efforts • Vigorous, vital action	• Not turning back • Reinforcing • Supporting • Consolidating • Restraining the mind	• Non-failing of mental state • Non-ending of mental state	• Sense of urgency • Anything that arouses energetic effort
13	Bare-desire (inclination/ intention)	An inclination for action or performance	Looking for an object to work on	Requiring an object	An object in need
14	Greed	Grasping of an object	• Creating attachment • Bonding through sticky/glue-like conditions	• Not letting go • Craving and clinging • Passion and lust • Selfishness • Ego	• Taking delight in things, activities, relationships, tasks, and goals that lead to bondage
15	Hatred	• Intensity, fierceness • Viciousness	• Putting things on fire • Spreading like fire • Burning up or devastating its own support	• Persecution • Aversion, anger • Disgust • Displeasure • Ego	• Conditions for aggravation or irritation

THE ELEMENTS OF SOUL

16	Delusion	• Ignorance • Not-knowing the reality of phenomena • Mental-blindness	• Creating illusion • Hiding the truth • Covering up the reality of phenomena	• Lack of understanding • Stupidity • Ego	• Delusion itself • Lack of wise attention
17	Restlessness	• Mental anxiety • Lack of calmness • Lack of stillness • Disquiet	• Making the mind unsteady and wavering like wind generating waves on the surface of an ocean	• Impatience • Agitation • Irritation • Turmoil • Confusion, indecision	• Giving unwise attention to mental disturbances
18	Shamelessness	• Non-apprehension about doing bad things • Immorality	• Making the mind do sinful, wicked, or immoral acts	• Lack of dread or anxiety about immorality • Wildness • Unruliness	• Lack of respect, honor, or reverence for oneself
19	Moral recklessness	• Apathy for misconduct • Apathy for doing bad things	• Making the mind do sinful, wicked, or immoral acts	• No moral caution • Not caring about or not shying away from unwholesomeness	• Lack of respect, honor, or reverence for oneself
20	Conceit	• Self-importance • Pride, haughtiness	• Glorifying or praising the self • Making arrogant	• Vanity • Intoxication • A desire to advertise oneself	• Greed without justification • Delusion
21	Envy	• Resentment about others' successes, achievements, and progress	• Making the mind dissatisfied and unhappy	• Disliking or distaste • Boredom or aversion due to others' successes	• Others' upper hand, achievements, victories, successes, progress, growth, or attainments
22	Remorse	• Regret about doing something wrong • Neglecting	• Making the mind sorrowful and mournful	• Repentance or guilt • Worry • Feeling of sorrow about doing wrong	• Not doing what ought to be done or doing what ought not to be done • Regrettable actions

APPENDIX C

23	Superstitiousness	• Wrong Views • Unjustifiable interpretation of things and phenomena	• Presuming, assuming, or supposing • Believing	• Beliefs • Unwise interpretations • Assumptions • Unhealthy religiousness • Personalized philosophies and -isms	• Lack of willingness to experience the truth or face reality • Lack of inclination towards wisdom • Evading reality
24	Suspicion	• Uncertainty • Inability to trust • Lack of desire to think through	• Wavering or vacillating • Making uncertain	• Lack of firmness • Indecisiveness • Changing camps	• Not giving wise attention to matters of doubt • Deciding without proper understanding
25	Sloth	• Stiffness • Lack of driving energy	• Removing mental energy	• Subsiding of mind • Lack of urgency and lack of energy when combined with torpor	• Lack of thinking • Giving unwise attention to boredom, monotony, and loneliness
26	Torpor	• Unwieldiness • Morbidity	• Choking the mind	• Sleepiness, laziness, and lethargy • Lack of urgency and lack of energy when combined with sloth	• Lack of thinking • Giving unwise attention to boredom, monotony, and loneliness
27	Avarice	• Hiding • Not sharing one's fortunes and successes with others	• Making sharing with others hard to stomach	• Stinginess, lack of generosity • Covetousness	• One's fortunes and successes
28	Non-greed	• Non-grasping • Non-sticking • Desirelessness	• Not attaching to an object • Non-clinging	• Letting go • Non-craving • Non-clinging • Non-attachment • Generosity • Unselfishness • Renunciation	• Not taking delight in things, activities, relationships, tasks, and goals that lead to greed

29	Non-hatred	• Lack of fierceness • Lack of resistance • Lack of opposition	Removing all types of irritation, frustration, annoyance, anger, and over-enthusiasm	• Loving-kindness • Sociability • Agreeableness • Amity • Gentleness • Friendliness • Calmness, softness, coolness, and pleasant appearance	• Seeing others as worthy of kindness and compassion • Recollecting the perfect accountability of the laws of karma
30	Mindfulness	• Presence of mind • Present-moment awareness • Steadiness and fullness of attention • Passive, relaxed, impartial, silent, receptive, and deepening observation	• Eliminating forgetfulness of the present moment • Remembering • Recollecting • Awakening • Stabilizing attention on an object by not drifting away from it • Minding an object of attention	• Facing and guarding an object of attention • Meditation • Awareness	• Strong, stable perception • Mindful contemplation of the phenomena of body-mind-consciousness
31	Conscience	• Disgust for misconduct • A sense of morality • Scrupulousness • Being principle-driven • Being ethical	Making mind not do sinful, immoral, or unethical things	• Modesty • Caring about or shying away from unwholesomeness • Moral caution • Civilized and cultured nature • Grace and reverence	Respect, honor, reverence for the self
32	Shame	• Apprehension for misconduct • A sense of morality • Scrupulousness • Being principle-driven • Being ethical	Making mind not do sinful, immoral, or unethical things	• Modesty • Caring about or shying away from unwholesomeness • Moral caution • Civilized and cultured nature	Respect, honor, reverence for others

APPENDIX C

#					
33	Faith	• Trust • Confidence	• Clarifying • Illuminating • Purifying the belief	• Firm decision • Clarity • Unshakable confidence	Experiential understanding of the 'subject or object' of faith
34 & 35	Tranquility of mind-body	Calming of disturbances and agitation	• Crushing and quieting disturbances • Destroying stress and distress • Removing restlessness and worry	• Stillness • Coolness • Peacefulness, quietness • Serenity • Heavenly delight • Dawning of bliss	• Uplifting happiness • Concentration • Insight related to body-mind-consciousness
36 & 37	Lightness of mind-body	Diminishing of heaviness	• Crushing heaviness • Removing sloth and torpor	• Nimbleness • Non-sluggishness	• Concentration • Insight related to body-mind-consciousness
38 & 39	Flexibility of mind-body	Diminishing of rigidity	• Crushing rigidity • Removing superstitiousness and conceit	• Non-resistance • Lack of stubbornness and obstinacy • Suppleness	• Concentration • Insight related to body-mind-consciousness
40 & 41	Pliability of mind-body	Diminishing of unworkability of mind	Crushing and quieting unworkability of mind	• Success in making something an object of mind • Profitable application of mind	• Concentration • Insight related to body-mind-consciousness
42 & 43	Skillfulness of mind-body	• Proficiency • Healthiness • Fitness	Crushing unhealthiness and disability	Absence of disability	• Concentration • Insight related to body-mind-consciousness
44 & 45	Rectitude of mind-body	• Directness • Uprightness	Crushing indirectness	Absence of impurities such as dishonesty, evasiveness, roundabout-ness, cleverness, smartness, and crookedness	• Concentration • Insight related to body-mind-consciousness

#				
46	Equanimity	• Neutrality of mind • Being in the middle • Non-reaction	• Neutralizing • Liberating from craving and aversion • Transcending pleasure and pain, joy and sorrow • Seeing all beings as equal including oneself	• Balance of mind • Disinterestedness of mind (not indifference) • Lack of greed, hatred • Absence of craving and aversion • Non-attachment • Middle-ness • Egolessness	• Mindfulness, concentration, and non-reaction • Maturing of loving-kindness, compassion, and gladness • Recollection of the laws of karma • Not taking delight in anything that lead to greed or hatred
47	Compassion	Inclination for removing others' suffering	Making it possible to see suffering in others Not being able to overlook others' suffering	• Non-meanness • Absence of cruelty • Making oneself peaceful	Seeing others as beings who are suffering (in the ultimate sense)
48	Gladness	Feelings of happiness, joy, and cheerfulness about the success of others	Eradicating jealousy and envy towards others' success	• Absence of irritation • Absence of aversion	Noticing and appreciating others' successes
49	Noble action	Unconditional non-wrongdoing by action	Shying away from or minimizing the generation of bad karma	Deliberate abstinence from wrong action	• Noble faith • Resolution • A sense of urgency for attaining mental perfection • A sense of contentment • Distaste for mundane living or wrongdoing
50	Noble speech	Unconditional non-wrongdoing by speech	Shying away from or minimizing the generation of bad karma	Deliberate abstinence from wrong speech	• Noble faith • Resolution • A sense of urgency for attaining mental perfection • Distaste for mundane living or wrongdoing

APPENDIX C

51	Noble occupation	Unconditional non-wrongdoing by occupation	Shying away from or minimizing the generation of bad karma	Deliberate abstinence from wrong occupation	• Noble faith in spiritual practices • Resolution • A sense of urgency for attaining mental perfection • A sense of contentment • Distaste for mundane living or wrongdoing
52	Non-delusion	• Penetration of the intrinsic nature of reality • Mental illumination • Knowledge of ultimate reality • Complete absence of ignorance	• Illuminating an object of investigation to the ultimate depth by piercing it • Exposing the truth as it is • Shaking off delusion • Eliminating superstition and religiousness • Enlightening mind	• Non-confusion • Wisdom • Egolessness • Pure understanding • Pure knowledge • Clear comprehension • Purification of views • Mental perfection • Enlightenment	• Giving wise-attention • Penetrating insight • Established mindfulness

Notes

This book is primarily based on my study of the following five sources and the realization of the various teachings that they describe. If paragraphs in *The Elements of Soul* should have been annotated, but were missed, in such cases the reader should refer to these five main sources, which alphabetically include:
- Access to Insight website: accesstoinsight.org.
- Analayo. *Satipatthana: The Direct Path to Realization.* Birmingham, UK: Windhorse Publications, 2004.
- Bodhi, Bhikkhu. *A Comprehensive Manual of Abhidhamma.* Onalaska, WA: Pariyatti Publications, 1999.
- Nanamoli, Bhikkhu. *Visuddhimagga: The Path of Purification.* Onalaska, WA: Pariyatti Publications, 1999.
- Rainbow Body Network website: rainbowbody.net/HeartMind/Yogasutra.htm.

I am solely responsible for all interpretations and extrapolations presented in my own work. Any faults, misrepresentations, or inadequacies should be considered the outcome of my limited understanding of these sources.

Preface

1. Roughly 2,500 years ago, Buddha was born as Gautama, a royal Indian prince in northern India. As a young prince, he grew disenchanted with leading a life of luxury and at age 29 he renounced royalty and became a wandering ascetic. He practiced extreme austerities in the forest for six years, defied fear, and surpassed the accomplishments of his spiritual teachers, but he wasn't enlightened until he abandoned austerity and adopted the so-called "middle way" (the way of moderation). Soon after (about one year later), he was enlightened to the truth of suffering, impermanence, and non-self. After enlightenment, he preached for roughly 45 years until his death. His disciples included people from all walks of life, including kings and members of his renounced family. His teachings were pragmatic and mainly consisted of developing virtuous conduct, the four noble truths, and the eightfold path. These teachings were systematically preserved in the form of more than 1,000 discourses in the Pali Canon (the Tipitaka). For further reading, visit accesstoinsight.org/ptf/buddha.html. Also see Nanamoli, 2001.

    Roughly 2000 years ago, an India sage named Patanjali (not to be confused with the inventor of yoga), wrote a compendium of ancient, pre-existing oral yoga teachings, which became known as *The Yoga Sutras*. These are a collection of 195 spiritual aphorisms divided into four *padas* (chapters) that describe the path of yoga for the attainment of mental perfection. *The Yoga Sutras* are the oldest written form describing the yogic practices of non-grasping and meditation. For further reading, see Roche and McNally. Also visit rainbowbody.net/HeartMind/Yogasutra.htm.

Chapter 1: What Is Soul?

1. The number of material elements, mental elements, and types of consciousness are derived from Abhidhamma Pitaka, a division of the Pali Canon, which is widely known as the collection of the Buddha's higher teachings. Although Abhidhamma does not

NOTES

talk about soul, like this book it is concerned with understanding reality through experience in a phenomenological and psychological way. For further reading, see Bodhi.

2. If you look at consciousness as that which has the single characteristic of cognizing an object, then you would not want to classify it into various types. However, if you want to signify the fact that there are momentary acts of cognition performed by a series of consciousnesses and not by a single consciousness, then it becomes necessary to look at consciousness as a stream of various types. It also facilitates understanding consciousness as a transient phenomenon. Depending upon the method of delineation, there can be 89 or 121 types. Bodhi: p. 29.
3. There are 24 conditional relations between various ultimate realities, which give rise to various experiences. How this happens will be explained in the sequel to this book, *Soul Mechanics*.
4. Here, intrinsic nature means the recurring (periodic) chemical properties, or atomic number, or patterns or trends in atomic radius, ionization energy, and electronegativity of the elements, or the electron configurations in the valence shell of an element.
5. Bodhi: p. 78.
6. These four criteria have been proposed by Buddhist commentators to reveal the nature of any ultimate reality. Bodhi: p. 29.
7. Bodhi: p. 136 and p. 144.
8. Bodhi: pp. 144–5.
9. Bodhi: pp. 235–6 and pp. 246–250.

Chapter 2: What Is Not Soul?

1. According to Abhidhamma philosophy, the four ultimate realities are: consciousness, mental factors, matter, and nirvana (enlightenment). Mental factors are similar to the mental elements that are known collectively as mind in *The Elements of Soul*. Source: Bodhi: p. 27.

Chapter 3: What Is Beyond Soul?

1. According to the glossary of Pali terms on the Access to Insight website, parinirvana means total unbinding, the complete cessation of five aggregates (matter, feeling, perception, mental formations, and consciousness) that occurs upon the death of a fully enlightened person (*arahant*). The main difference between nirvana and parinirvana is the respective presence or absence of the live body of a fully enlightened master. Source website: accesstoinsight.org/glossary.html#pq. Also see Buddha's discourse Parinibbana Sutta 6.15. Website: accesstoinsight.org/tipitaka/sn/sn06/sn06.015.than.html.

Chapter 4: How Soul Works

1. *Classical (Newtonian) mechanics tell us about the behavior of macroscopic physical objects, ranging from pebbles to planets ...* The term "classical mechanics" was introduced in the scientific world in the 20th century. It is used to refer collectively to mathematical physics, developed by Isaac Newton and other 17th–20th century scientists; Lagrangian mechanics; Hamiltonian mechanics; and Albert Einstein's mechanics. For further reading, see Sussman and Wisdom with Mayer.

Quantum mechanics tell us about the behavior of microscopic physical objects, ranging from molecules and atoms, to electrons and strings ... Quantum mechanics differs from classical mechanics in that it considers not only the point particle of very small size (such as an electron), but also the spin of particles. Quantum mechanics was developed in the first half of 20th century by scientists like Albert Einstein, Werner Heisenberg, Max Planck, Erwin Schrödinger, Niels Bohr, Paul Dirac, and the likes. It goes beyond classical mechanics by describing the workings of physical systems at the atomic level and beyond. The most important aspect of quantum mechanics is its ability to address the dual nature of matter, which is both particle-like and wave-like. In classical mechanics, Newton's second law of motion can be used to obtain the determinate position of a particle. According to quantum mechanics, there is no such thing as a determinate or certain position of a particle, but only the wave function of the particle. A wave function provides only the statistical likelihood of the position of a particle in space. This is also known as the uncertainty principle, which states that there is no way to know the position and velocity of an electron at the same time. See Griffiths, 1987: pp. 1–5.

Popularly they are searching for a theory of everything (TOE) ... There are four known fundamental forces in nature: gravity, electromagnetism, strong nuclear force, and weak nuclear force. Classical mechanics (and general relativity) can describe the workings of gravity and quantum mechanics can describe the workings of other three forces. But neither can describe the workings of all the forces. Scientists are searching for a new theory that will unify all the forces. This theory is known as the theory of everything. Sources: Griffiths, 2004: pp. 46–8; and Weinberg: pp. 200–5.

2. Kaku: p. 236.
3. Here, the word "conserve" is used in a technical sense (the law of conservation of energy) and not in a vernacular sense, as in avoiding waste.
4. *Even great physicists like Isaac Newton and Albert Einstein firmly believed that the universe ran like a clock* ... Kaku: pp. 242, 292–3. Einstein's statement, *"God does not throw dice,"* is cited in Kaku: p. 58.
5. Niels Bohr's statement, "Don't tell God what to do!" is cited in Rae: p. 22. Some doubt the historical accuracy of this statement. Walter Isaccson quotes Einstein, "I have earned the right to be wrong," in *Einstein: His Life and Universe*: p. 515. Elsewhere there are slightly different versions of this utterance.
6. See note 2.

Chapter 5: Soul Intelligence

1. See Bibliography for details on the books of evolutionary biologist Richard Dawkins, D.Phil., child psychiatrist Jim Tucker,

M.D., molecular biologist A.G. Cairns-Smith, Ph.D., physicist Michio Kaku, Ph.D., zoologist and journalist Matt Ridley, D. Phil., astrobiologist and astrophysicist David Darling, Ph.D., and futurist Ray Kurzweil.

2. Definitions of intelligence used here were derived from the works of psychologist Alfred Binet, Ph.D., inventor of the IQ test; educational psychologist Sir Cyril Burt; educational psychologist Linda Gottfredson; psychologist and psychometrician Robert Sternberg; psychologist David Weshler, the creator of intelligence scales; and educator Howard Gardner, Ph.D. For further reading, see Neisser et al: pp. 77–101; and Acton. Website: personalityresearch.org/intelligence.html.

3. *The most widely known method is based on psychometrics...* Gardner, 2000: pp. 11–3. For further reading, see Furr and Bacharach.

   Howard Gardner, a well-known intelligence theorist from Harvard University, believes that there is no such thing as "general" intelligence (g) or IQ that can fully describe cognitive ability ... Gardner: pp. 13 and 22.

4. Sources: Kaku: p. 112 and Kurzweil, 1999: p. 69.

5. Sources: Kaku: pp. 24 and 123; Kurzweil, 1999: pp. 20–5 and 33; and Kurzweil, 2005: p. 25.

6. *Concepts of emotional intelligence (which is popularly known as EQ) were introduced, developed, and...* Goleman: pp. 34–6; Payne; and Greenspan, 1990.

   In fact, seeds of EQ were planted... Bradberry and Greaves: pp. 24–5.

   Edward Thorndike, who conceived of the idea...Bradberry: p. 24. Also, see Plucker.

   Howard Gardner introduced the model of multiple ... Gardner: pp. 33–5.

   However it wasn't until Daniel Goleman ... Goleman: pp. ix–x, and Gardner: p. 10.

NOTES

7. *Some of the models, such as the competency-based model proposed by Goleman, are criticized as being pop psychology ...* Mayer, Roberts, and Barsade: pp. 507–36.
8. Locke: pp. 425-31. Also see Eysenck.
9. *The term itself was reportedly coined by Danah Zohar...* See Zohar and Marshall.

    Other thinkers, among them... See Buzan. Also see Noble: pp. 1–29, and King.

    oward Gardner excluded SQ from his theory... Gardner: pp. 60 and 65–6.
10. *However, these laws break down beyond ...* For further details, see Imamura.
11. Earth is surrounded by magnetic field that makes a compass needle move in a particular direction. Earth's gravitational field gives rise to gravitational force at a particular location. In this sense, I am suggesting that we are permeated by the field of intelligence, due to which we experience volitional forces that are responsible for our mental actions.
12. Sources: Kaku: p. 104; Searle: pp. 88–91; Kurzweil, 1999: p. 69; Kurzweil, 2005: pp. 8–9, 25–6; and Penrose, 1989: pp. 526–31.
13. Hydrogen is thought to have formed due to big bang nucleogenesis. Hydrogen is by far the most abundant element in the universe, accounting for about 90 percent of atoms and 75 percent of mass in the universe. It is the dominant constituent of the most abundant matter in the universe, plasma. Its molecule, H_2, is also the most abundant molecule in the universe. The four most abundant elements in human body are hydrogen, oxygen, carbon, and nitrogen. These elements exist because of hydrogen and various types of nucleosynthesis (thermonuclear fusion and fission) that created them. Clayton: pp. 11–2.
14. See Russell. Also see Barras.
15. Kaku: p. 104 and Penrose, 1989: p. 526.
16. Details on the death of Ludwig Boltzmann come from Kaku: p. 265.

Biographical details on Hans Berger are drawn from the website: chem.ch.huji.ac.il/history/berger.html.

Details on the death of Edwin Armstrong come from the obituary column "Milestones" in *Time* (February 8, 1954).

Biographical details on George Eastman come from The NNDB Tracker website: nndb.com/people/980/000086722/#FN1.

17. Kaku: pp. 106–7.
18. Kaku: p. 198.

Chapter 6: Soul Meditation

1. Derived from Nanamoli, 1999: p. 261.
2. Derived from vipassana meditation practice, as taught by S.N. Goenka. For further reading, visit the Vipassana Meditation website: dhamma.org.

Chapter 7: Exploring the Ultimate Building Blocks of Matter

1. According to the molecular or kinetic theory of matter, matter is simply made of molecules that are constantly moving and bouncing off each other. According to the atomic theory of matter, matter is made of atoms, which in turn are made of electrons, protons, and neutrons. According to the modern universal theory of matter, matter is made of quarks and gluons, and thus it is essentially "matter fields" or "scalar fields." According to string theory, matter is not really made of any particles at all, but of vibrating strings. The Bureau International defines matter as "substance."
2. Here the word "entropy' is used to indicate the amount of disorder or randomness, or wasted energy for attaining equilibrium in an isolated system. An in-depth study of entropy is recommended to avoid misunderstanding.
3. A basic understanding of the four essential material elements can arise by studying some of their salient features, which include the following:

NOTES

A) Earth, water, fire, and air are distinct elements because they bear their own characteristics. However, they cannot be separated from each other. None can be discovered or demonstrated as an individual element. They always arise together and serve as a common base for the occurrence of matter such as a rock or a human body.

B) Taken together, the four essential elements are supported by earth, held together by water, maintained by fire, and distended by air. Earth is held together by water, maintained by fire, and distended by air, so that matter is neither scattered nor dissipated, but manifests as small, big, tall, short, rough, rigid, hard, and so on. Water is founded on earth, maintained by fire, and distended by air, so it does neither trickles nor flows away, but provides cohesion, continuity, and flow. Fire is established on earth, held together by water element, and distended by air, so it provides warmth and maintains the body. Fire prevents the animate body from rotting. Air is founded on earth element, held together by water, and maintained by fire, so it does not allow the body to collapse, but makes it stand erect, walk, wiggle, and sit, and otherwise moves the body parts.

C) Although they do not exist without each other, the four essential elements are found neither inside nor outside of each other. They mutually condition each other and assist each other in fulfilling their functions.

D) The differences in material things are not due to differences in the characteristics of the essential elements, but to a difference in the capability and quality of the essential material elements that have arisen. Mt. Fuji and the Colorado River are different not because there is a greater quantity of earth in soil and rock or because there is a lesser quantity of earth in rapidly flowing water. Mt. Fuji has an excess of earth element in capability and in quality.

Similarly, hot water does not have fire in excess quantity. Nor does cold water lack fire. Hot water is hot because of excessive capability or quality of fire. Cold water is cold because of less capability or quality of fire. In brief, various material things exist because of differences in the capability or quality of four elements and not in their quantity.

4. See "On Nature," the poetic work of Empedocles describing his teachings. Stanford Encyclopedia of Philosophy website: plato.stanford.edu/entries/empedocles/#1.
5. See "Plato's Timaeus: Physics," Stanford Encyclopedia of Philosophy website: plato.stanford.edu/entries/plato-timaeus/#8.
6. Arikha: pp. 3–6. Also see Garrison.
7. "Kayagata-sati Sutta: Mindfulness Immersed in the Body," MN 119, translated by Thanissaro Bhikkhu. Website: accesstoinsight.org/tipitaka/mn/mn.119.than.html.
8. See Miyamoto.
9. Svoboda: pp. 29–39.
10. Popular modern examples of the four elements include the comic book series *The Fantastic Four* (Marvel Comics, written by Stan Lee and illustrated by Jack Kirby) and the movie *Fantastic Four* (Fox 2005, directed by Tim Story); the Harry Potter book series written by J.K. Rowling (*Harry Potter and the Sorcerer's Stone*, Scholastic 1998) and movie series (Warner Brothers). Also see Heslewood.
11. The standard model is a theory of elementary particles that make up all the matter in the universe. More precisely, it is a theory about the interaction between particles of matter—a means to describe all the known forces in nature as one common force (aka the super force). At present, this theory is considered incomplete because it does not include gravity. For further reading on this topic, see Griffiths, 1987: pp. 46–8.
12. Kaku: pp. 234–5; Greene, 2003: pp. 13–20; Greene, 2004: pp. 328–75; and Penrose, 2005: pp. 884–900. For additional information on string theory, see "The Elegant Universe," *Nova*. Public Broadcasting System website: pbs.org/wgbh/nova/elegant; and The Official String Theory website: superstringtheory.com.

NOTES

13. See Capra.
14. Kaku: p. 236. Also see "The Elegant Universe" and The Official String Theory website.
15. Kaku: p. 302.
16–17. Kaku: pp. 264–5 and pp. 296–7.
18. Kaku: p. 287–90.
19. See "What Is a Cell?" National Center for Biotechnology Information website: ncbi.nlm.nih.gov/About/primer/genetics_cell.html.
20. See Weiss. Also see Wright.
21. See O'Reilly.
22. Kaku: p. 270.
23. Ibid.
24. Derived from Bodhi: p. 246.
25. Iannone: p. 30. Also see Potter.
26. For detailed reading, explore *Space and Time: Inertial Frames at* plato.stanford.edu/entries/spacetime-iframes.
27. Based on Kaku: pp. 247, 250–2, and 282. For further reading, see Greene, 2004.
28. The term "non-concrete matter" is derived from Bodhi: pp. 240–1.
29. See "General Relativity," *Einstein Online*. Website: einstein-online.info/en/spotlights/gr/index.html.
30. Derived from Bodhi: pp. 236–42.

Chapter 8: Exploring Consciousness

1. In the past, René Descartes (16–17th century), who is sometimes called the father of modern philosophy, defined consciousness as ideas, imaginings, and perceptions in space and time. Philosophers from the 18th–20th century generally related consciousness to relations, processes, and thoughts. Modern philosophers attribute consciousness to thoughts, moods, sensations, perceptions, dreams, self-awareness, and being awake and responsive to the environment. Some psychologists attribute

consciousness to that which arises due to the language of high complexity.

For most of the 20th century, although the research related to consciousness was banned in the scientific psychology circles, consciousness was studied as a topic of "attention." (source: susan-blackmore.co.uk/books/consciousness/cons.htm) Evolutionary biologists approach consciousness as the subject of "adaptation." Theoretical neurobiologists define consciousness as "supremely functional adaptation." Some philosophers from the field of cognitive sciences define consciousness as that which passes the Turing test (Searle: pp. 70–4) or the mirror test (source: sciencedaily.com/articles/m/mirror_test.htm). Some modern physicists consider consciousness to be the subject of quantum entanglement and superposition. Physicist Roger Penrose explains consciousness in his orchestrated objective reduction theory through mathematics, physics, and anesthesia as a non-algorithmic and non-computable function of the brain. It appears that he relates wave function collapse in microtubes of neurons to consciousness. For further reading, see Penrose, 1994: pp. 161 and 350–377, Penrose, 1989: pp. 521–5, Blackmore, 1989.

2. Due to its vastness and complexity, the rationale behind the composition of mental elements for each type of consciousness will be discussed in *Soul Mechanics,* the upcoming sequel to this book.
3. Due to its wide scope and implications, the phenomena of birth and death consciousness (and the boundary conditions of the human lifespan) will be discussed in detail in *Soul Mechanics,* the upcoming sequel to this book.
4–5. Derived from Bodhi: pp. 151–6.

Chapter 9: Exploring the Ultimate Building Blocks of Mind

1. Neuroscientists believe that mind is same as the brain, which thinks, perceives, wills, and feels. Philosophers believe that mind is a non-material entity separate from the body and it is that

which permits a person to think, love, hate, and so forth. Neurophysiologists consider mind as a functional entity related only to the existence of the brain and to the brain's reception of sensory inputs. Cognitive neuroscientists attribute mind to the activity of neural cells. Some philosophers, mystics, and theological thinkers define mind as the essence of a person, as spirit or soul. For further reading, see Searle.
2. How memory is stored and retrieved, why the brain sleeps and dreams, what is time (as perceived by the brain), what the baseline activity of the brain is, how to develop an artificial brain (AI), what consciousness is, what an emotion is, where we (and our thoughts) come from, what the beginning of evolution is, creation vs. evolution, nature vs. nurture, and what the secrete of life is—these are some of our current scientific mysteries.
3. This description of all the mental elements is derived from my studies of Visuddhimagga (source: Nanamoli, 1999) and the Abhidhamma treatises (source: Bodhi), and from my own insights.
4. Derived from Bodhi: pp. 78–90.

Chapter 10: The Universal Mind

1. Derived from Analayo: p. 158.
2. In Jainism, Judaism, some forms of Orthodox Christianity and Catholicism, Buddhism, and Zen Buddhism, as well as in the religious yoga tradition, painful ascetic practices are undertaken, such as no personal ownership, extreme fasting, self-denial, extreme physical exercises, and forced celibacy, under the assumption that they will burn up the effects of unwholesome past deeds and bring about salvation, purification, and retribution.

Chapter 12: The Unwholesome Mind

1. Although mysticism can take a practitioner beyond religious doctrine by facilitating exploration of the esoteric aspects of spirituality, mysticism can become a hindrance to enlightenment—especially if the equality complex is not understood clearly.

I humbly urge practitioners of various mystical traditions, such as Vedanta Hinduism, Kabbalism, and Sufism, as well as Christian mysticism, to go beyond the final threshold of the equality complex and attain perfection.

Chapter 13: The Wholesome Mind

1. By far, confusing belief with faith is the biggest mistake that the majority of religious practitioners make. In fact, many of them go to the extent of equating faith with religion. This is also the costliest mistake made by human beings. It would not be very difficult to prove that human beings have fought more wars due to *belief* (racial, social, cultural, or religious) than due to any other reason.
2. Note that tranquility Tr1 (element 34) refers to tranquility of body, however, it is not necessarily related to the physical body, but to the entire group (a body) of 19 wholesome elements. Tranquility Tr2 (element 35) refers to tranquility of mind which means tranquility is a distinct mental element. So is the case with the other five pairs. Together, the 12 mental elements 34–45 form six pairs, which always arise together as a group.

Chapter 14: The Divine Mind

1. Many theological thinkers believe that divinity is an attribute only of a godly figure having supernatural powers. They also believe divinity is an entity, such as a godhead, a deity, or a supreme being (aka the Almighty) that resides beyond the human realm. Some theological thinkers also use this word in terms of divine intervention.

Chapter 15: The Noble Mind

1. These three elements are specifically derived from three elements of abstinence listed in Bodhi: p. 79.
2. Derived from Fischer.
3. Frady: pp. 102–3 and pp. 123–4.

NOTES

Chapter 16: The Perfect Mind

1. As made obvious by Einstein's famous equation, $E=MC^2$ (where M equals the mass of a particle and C equals the speed of light), a tremendous amount of energy can be released by an atom (the core) of uranium when it is subjected to a nuclear fission reaction.

Chapter 17: Developing an Intelligent Attitude

1. The ten virtues are derived from Patanjali's Yoga Sutras. For further study, visit rainbowbody.net/HeartMind/Yogasutra.htm.
2. Acharya Rajnish was an Indian mystic who preached sexual liberation and sexual *tantras* (techniques) as a means of spiritual growth. His teachings may have adversely impacted the spiritual quest of many innocent followers. There are many tantric and yogic practices (such as yama marga, maithuna, Shiva-Shaktism, and yogic sexual union) that ignorantly assume sexual activity as a means of liberation, thereby encouraging sexual overindulgence.
3. In religious yoga traditions, such as Darshan Yoga and Om Yoga Sansthan, among others, Ishwar pranidhana, the *niyama* (lifestyle/virtue) mentioned in Patanjali's Yoga Sutras (which is written in Sanskrit), is misunderstood as surrendering to God or finding shelter in God. This misunderstanding has occurred because the ancient Sanskrit word "Ishwar" means "God." Similar misunderstanding is present in almost all religious traditions that follow religious texts written in ancient languages.

Chapter 18: Developing Intelligent Senses

1. If you are a beginner, you must avoid touching the genitals while practicing this meditation so that you can maintain non-reaction throughout the session.
2. Here, the word "religiously" is used to convey the seriousness of practice. Massage therapists must also practice the other meditations given in this book so that they can maintain purity of thought and purity of action while working with their clients.

3. For information on entrainment, as it is generally thought of, visit Jonathan Goldman's Healing Sounds website: healingsounds.com/articles/sonic-entrainment.asp. In this book, the idea of entrainment is taken further and deeper by instructing the practitioner to focus on gaps of silence embedded in the sound track.

Chapter 19: Developing an Intelligent Body

1. Out-of-body experiences (OBE) derived from taking psychedelic drugs or experiencing traumatic near-death experiences, extreme dehydration, dreams, and such are generally rooted in ignorance or intoxication. An authentic OBE is the spiritual experience of transcending the body—meaning, going beyond bodily attachments.

Chapter 20: Developing an Intelligent Mind

1. These four practices are derived from my realization of the teachings described in Abhidhamma (see Bodhi) and Visuddhimagga (see Nanamoli).

Chapter 21: Developing an Intelligent Heart

1. These four practices are derived from my realization of the teachings described in Visuddhimagga (see Nanamoli).

Epilogue

1. This statement is attributed to Joko Charlotte Beck, a Zen Buddhist teacher. Some people wonder why terms such as "enlightened master," "the Buddha," and so on are used. They are used for the sake of communication, just as we use the words "I" and "you" even though we may know that there is no such thing. In reality, there is no "person" attaining enlightenment. Impersonality is, in fact, the mark of enlightenment.
2. Buddha's daily routine was extraordinary. He spent most of his time teaching and meditating. He would meditate during the very early hours of the morning (2 a.m. to 6 a.m.) either while sitting, walking, or by contemplating enlightenment. He slept no more

than two hours each night. According to some accounts, he slept just one hour a day. See Nanamoli.

3. According to Merriam-Webster's Online Dictionary, the word "omniscient" means "having infinite understanding or complete knowledge." Considering this meaning, it is obvious that a person (who is finite) cannot become omniscient. Buddha himself never explicitly stated that he was omniscient. He, in fact, considered the idea of omniscience to be irrelevant and taught his disciples instead to focus on the conditionality of all phenomena. He also stated that it is not possible to know everything simultaneously. See Majjhima Nikaya, Sutta 90. Website: accesstoinsight.org/tipitaka/mn/mn.090.than.html. Also see Thomas: p. 213.

* * *

Bibliography

Acton, G. Scott, Ph.D. "Intelligence," online article (updated January 1999). Great Ideas in Personality Website: personalityresearch.org/intelligence.html.

Analayo. *Satipatthana: The Direct Path to Realization.* Birmingham, UK: Windhorse Publications, 2003.

Arikha, Noga. *Passions and Tempers: A History of the Humours.* New York, NY: Ecco Press, 2007.

Bar-On, Reuven, Maree, J.G., and Maurice, Jesse E., editors. *Educating People to Be Emotionally Intelligent.* Westport, CT: Praeger Publishers, 2007.

Barras, Colin. "Smart Amoebas Reveal Origins of Primitive Intelligence," *New Scientist*, vol. 16, no. 11 (October 2008). Website: newscientist.com/article/dn15068.

Blackmore, Susan. Website: susanblackmore.co.uk.

Blackmore, Susan. *Consciousness: An Introduction:* New York, NY: Oxford University Press, 2004

Bodhi, Bhikkhu. *A Comprehensive Manual of Abhidhamma.* Onalaska, WA: Pariyatti Publications, 1999.

Bradberry, Travis and Greaves Jean. *Emotional Intelligence Quickbook: Everything You Need to Know.* San Diego, CA: TalentSmart, 2003.

Buzan, Tony. *The Power of Spiritual Intelligence: Ten Ways to Tap into Your Spiritual Genius.* London, UK: Thorsons, 2001.

Cairns-Smith, A.G. *Evolving the Mind: On the Nature of Matter and the Origin of Consciousness.* Cambridge, UK: Cambridge University Press, 1998.

Capra, Fritjof. *The Turning Point: Science, Society, and the Rising Culture.* New York, NY: Bantam, 1984.

Chopra, Ananda S. "Ayurveda," from *Medicine Across Cultures: History and Practice of Medicine in Non-western Cultures,* edited by Helaine Selin and Hugh Shapiro. Norwell, MA: Kluwer Academic Publishers, 2003.

Clayton, Donald. *Handbook of Isotopes in the Cosmos: Hydrogen to Gallium.* Cambridge, UK: Cambridge University Press, 2003.

Darling, David. *Life Everywhere: The Maverick Science of Astrobiology.* New York, NY: Basic Books, 2002.

Darling, David. *Zen Physics: The Science of Death, The Logic of Reincarnation.* New York, NY: HarperCollins Publishers, 1996.

Dawkins, Richard. *The Extended Phenotype: The Long Reach of the Gene.* Revised edition. New York, NY: Oxford University Press, 1999.

Dawkins, Richard. *The Ancestor's Tale: A Pilgrimage to the Dawn of Evolution.* New York, NY: Houghton Mifflin, 2004.

Diggha Nikaya, Sutta 16. *Mahaparinibbana Sutta.* Website: accesstoinsight.org.

DiSalle, Robert. "Space and Time: Inertial Frames," *Stanford Encyclopedia of Philosophy.* Posted online March 2002. Website: plato.stanford.edu/entries/spacetime-iframes.

Empedocles. "On Nature," *Stanford Encyclopedia of Philosophy.* Website: plato.stanford.edu/entries/empedocles/#1.

Eysenck, Hans J. *Intelligence: A New Look.* New Brunswick, NJ: Transaction Publishers, 1998.

Fischer, Louis. *Gandhi: His Life and Message for the World.* Denver, CO: Mentor Books, 1954.

Frady, Marshall. *Martin Luther King, Jr.: A Life.* New York, NY: Viking Penguin, 2002.

Furr, R. Michael and Bacharach, Verne R. *Psychometrics: An Introduction.* Thousand Oaks, CA: Sage Publications, 2008.

Gardner, Howard. *Intelligence Reframed: Multiple Intelligences for the 21st Century.* New York, NY: Basic Books, 2000.

Garrison, Fielding H. *An Introduction to the History of Medicine: With Medical Chronology, Suggestions for Study, and Bibliographic Data.* Fourth edition. Philadelphia, PA: W.B. Saunders and Company, 1967.

Goldman, Jonathan. The Healing Sounds website: healingsounds.com.

Goleman, Daniel. *Emotional Intelligence: Why It Can Matter More Than IQ.* New York, NY: Bantam Books, 1995.

Greene, Brian. *The Elegant Universe: Superstrings, Hidden Dimensions, and the Quest for the Ultimate Theory.* New York, NY: W.W. Norton & Company, 2003.

Greene, Brian. *The Fabric of the Cosmos: Space, Time, and the Texture of Reality.* New York, NY: Alfred A. Knopf, 2004.

Greenspan, Stanley I. *The Development of the Ego: Implications for Personality Theory, Psychopathology, and the Psychotherapeutic Process.* Madison, CT: International Universities Press, 1990.

Greenspan, Stanley I. *The Essential Partnership: How Parents and Children Can Meet the Emotional Challenges of Infancy and Childhood.* New York, NY: Viking, 1989.

Griffiths, David J. *Introduction to Elementary Particles.* New York, NY: John Wiley & Sons, 1987.

Griffiths, David J. *Introduction to Quantum Mechanics.* Second edition. Upper Saddle River, NJ: Benjamin Cummings, 2004.

Heslewood, Juliet. *Earth, Air, Fire, and Water.* New York, NY: Oxford University Press, 1989.

Hertzig, Margaret E., M.D., and Farber, Ellen A., Ph.D., editors. *Annual Progress in Child Psychiatry and Child Development 1997*. New York, NY: Routledge, 1998.

Iannone, A. Pablo. *Dictionary of World Philosophy*. New York, NY: Routledge, 2001.

Imamura, James N. "Newton and Einstein," online article (accessed December 2008). University of Oregon Website: zebu.uoregon.edu/~imamura/talks/gravity_waves/newton.html.

Isaccson, Walter. *Einstein: His Life and Universe*. New York, NY: Simon and Schuster, 2007.

Kaku, Michio. *Physics of the Impossible: A Scientific Exploration into the World of Phasers, Force Fields, Teleportation, and Time Travel*. New York, NY: Doubleday, 2008.

King, David B. The Spiritual Intelligence Project Website: dbking.net/spiritualintelligence.

Kurzweil, Ray. *The Age of Spiritual Machines: When Computers Exceed Human Intelligence*. New York, NY: Viking, 1999.

Kurzweil, Ray. *The Singularity Is Near: When Humans Transcend Biology*. New York, NY: Viking Penguin, 2005.

Locke, Edwin A. "Why Emotional Intelligence Is an Invalid Concept," *Journal of Organizational Behavior*, vol. 26, no. 4 (April 2005): pp. 425-31.

Majjhima Nikaya, Sutta 90. *Kannakatthala Sutta*. Website: accesstoinsight.org.

Mayer, John D., Roberts, Richard D., and Barsade, Sigal G. "Human Abilities: Emotional Intelligence," *Annual Reviews of Psychology*, vol. 59 (January 2008): pp. 507-536.

Merriam-Webster Online Dictionary. Website: merriam-webster.com.

Miyamoto, Musashi, *A Book of Five Rings*. Website: miyamotomusashi.com/gorin.htm.

Nanamoli, Bhikkhu, *The Life of the Buddha: According to the Pali Canon*. Onaslaska, WA: Pariyatti Publishing, 2001.

Nanamoli, Bhikkhu. *Visuddhimagga: The Path of Purification*. Onaslaska, WA: Pariyatti Publications, 1999.

Neisser, Ulric, Boodoo, Gwyneth, Bouchard, Thomas J., Jr., Boykin, A. Wade, Brody, Nathan, Ceci, Stephen J., Halpern, Diane F., Loehlin, John C., Perloff, Robert, Sternberg, Robert J., Urbina, Susana. "Intelligence: Knowns and Unknowns," *American Psychologist*, vol. 51, no. 2 (February 1996): pp. 77-101.

Noble, Kathleen D. "Spiritual Intelligence: A New Frame of Mind," *Advanced Development Journal*, vol. 9 (2000): pp. 1-29.

Noble, Kathleen D. "Spiritual Intelligence: Global Perspectives," Consciousness Research Abstracts, *Journal of Consciousness Studies*, vol. 376 (2000).

Noble, Kathleen D. *Riding the Windhorse: Spiritual Intelligence and the Growth of the Self.* Cresskill, N.J.: Hampton Press, 2001.

O'Reilly, Deirdre, M.D. "Fetal Development," *MedlinePlus Medical Encyclopedia* (updated October 2007). U.S. National Library of Medicine and Public Health Website: www.nlm.nih.gov/medlineplus/ency/article/002398.htm.

Payne, Wayne L. "A Study of Emotion: Developing Emotional Intelligence," a 1985 doctoral thesis, The Union Institute. Website: eqi.org/payne.htm.

Penrose, Roger. *The Emperor's New Mind: Concerning Computers, Minds, and the Laws of Physics.* New York, NY: Oxford University Press, 1989.

Penrose, Roger. *Shadows of the Mind: A Search for the Missing Science of Consciousness.* New York, NY: Oxford University Press, 1994.

Penrose, Roger. *The Road to Reality: A Complete Guide to the Laws of the Universe.* New York, NY: Alfred A. Knopf, 2005.

Plucker, J. A. (Ed.). "Human Intelligence: Historical Influences, Current Controversies, Teaching Resources" (2003). Retrieved October 2008 from indiana.edu/~intell/.

Potter, Karl H., editor. *Indian Metaphysics and Epistemology: The Tradition of Nyaya-Vaisesika Up to Gangesa.* Princeton, NJ: Princeton University Press 1978.

Rae, Alastair. *Quantum Physics: Illusion or Reality?* Cambridge, UK: Cambridge University Press, 1984.

Ridley, Matt. *Genome: The Autobiography of Species in 23 Chapters.* New York, NY: HarperCollins Publishers, 2000.

Roche, Geshe Michael and McNally, Christie. *The Essential Yoga Sutra: Ancient Wisdom for Your Yoga.* New York, NY: Three Leaves Press, 2005.

Russell, Dale A. "Speculations on the Evolution of Intelligence in Multicellular Organisms," a paper presented at the Life in the Universe Conference held at National Ames Research Center in Moffet Field, California (June 19–20, 1979). Website: history.nasa.gov/CP-2156/ch4.3.htm.

Schwarz, Patricia. The Official String Theory Website: superstringtheory.com.

Searle, John R. *Mind: A Brief Introduction.* New York, NY: Oxford University Press, 2004.

Sussman, Gerald Jay and Wisdom, Jack with Mayer, Meinhard E. *Structures and Interpretation of Classical Mechanics.* Cambridge, MA: The MIT Press, 2001.

Sukys, Paul. *Lifting the Scientific Veil: Science Appreciation for the Nonscientist.* Lanham, MD: Ardsley House Publishers, 1999.

Svoboda, Robert. *Ayurveda: Life, Health, and Longevity.* Albuquerque, NM: The
Ayurvedic Press, 2004.

Thomas, Edward J. *The Life of Buddha as Legend and History.* New Delhi, India: Motilal Banarsidass Publishers, 1993.

Thorndike, R.K. "Intelligence and Its Uses," *Harper's Magazine*, vol. 140 (1920): pp.227-335.

Tucker, Jim B. *Life Before Life: A Scientific Investigation of Children's Memories of Previous Lives.* New York, NY: St. Martin's Press, 2005.

The Vipassana Meditation Website: dhamma.org.

Weinberg, Steven. *Dreams of a Final Theory: The Scientist's Search for the Ultimate Laws of Nature.* New York, NY: Pantheon, 1993.

Weiss, Achim. "Big Bang Nucleosynthesis: Cooking up the First Light Elements," online article (updated April 2006). Einstein Online Website: einstein-online.info/en/spotlights/BBN/index.html

Wright, Edward L. "Big Bang Nucleosynthesis," online article (2002–2004). Website: astro.ucla.edu/~wright/BBNS.html.

Zohar, Danah and Marshall, Ian. *Spiritual Intelligence: the Ultimate Intelligence.* London, UK: Bloomsbury Publishing, 1999.

Zohar, Danah and Marshall, Ian. *Spiritual Capital: Wealth We Can Live By.* San Francisco, CA: Berrett-Koehler Publishers, 2004.

* * *

Index

absolute, 49, 50, 85, 135-36, 152, 283-84
absorption, 56, 106, 147, 177
abstinence, 198, 211, 247-49
addiction, 179, 221, 275-76, 314
addiction-free, 303
affliction-free, 303
aggression, 194
agnosticism, 202
air, 34-35, 43, 108, 111, 121-23, 148, 292, 308, 335, 401
Akash, 136
alpha wave rhythm, 293
AM modulation, 33
AM/FM receiver, 33
Ancient Greeks, 123-24
anger, 40, 73, 92, 94, 107, 156, 165, 190, 207, 212-13, 241-44, 250-51, 312-13, 336, 343-44, 347-54, 356, 361
animosity, 176, 190, 241, 251, 353
anti-corruption, 250
anti-materialism, 120, 139
apathy, 189, 191, 195, 232, 235, 362
appreciative joy, 245, 357
Aristotle, 124
aromatherapy, 292
artificial intelligence (AI), 87
asceticism, 211, 213
Atma, 147
atom, 121, 125-26, 131-32, 407
attachment, 13-14, 50, 89, 138, 161, 182, 187, 200, 210, 224-25, 233, 311, 321
attention span, 295

austerity, 265-66, 278-79, 394
autonomous functions, 309
avarice, 205-06, 269
aversion, 45-6, 65, 109-10, 113-14, 163-66, 190-91, 198, 204-05, 221, 229, 245, 310, 343-44, 359
awareness, 4, 6, 19, 50, 56, 102, 110-11, 162, 204-05, 213-14, 216-18, 234, 325-33, 337-39
Ayurveda, 124
balance, 181, 194, 222, 229, 312, 323
bare desire, 181-84, 206
being, 19, 50, 71, 85, 152, 200, 276, 406
belief, 50-51, 223-25, 406
benevolence, 208
Berger, Hans, 93, 400
Big Bang Observer, 129
Big Bang, 87, 134, 136-37, 399, 417
biofeedback, 97-98
birth, 81, 144, 147, 404
blind devotion, 224
blind faith, 200
bliss, 176, 319, 330, 359, 361, 364
  liberating, 338
  momentary, 326-28
  pervading, 328-30
  showering, 328
  uplifting, 328-29
blood, 33, 130, 132-33
bodily-intimation, 36-37, 138

body, 11-14, 16, 61, 89, 111, 119-20, 124, 130, 132-33, 139, 146, 167, 211, 217, 257, 274-75, 288-91, 303-20, 327-28, 330
Bohr, Niels, 78, 396
Boltzmann, Ludwig, 93, 399
bones, 34, 130, 309, 335
boredom, 110, 204-05, 222, 228, 245, 253
boundless space, 200
Brahman, 196-97
brain, 32-35, 61, 83, 87-88, 133, 148, 404-05
breath, 34, 106-13, 216-17, 315-18, 325-28, 330, 335
breath awareness, 107-12, 316, 325
breathing, 61, 106, 111, 289, 296, 315, 325
breath-taker, 111, 217
British empire, 252
Buddha, 5, 24, 124, 240, 355, 363, 365, 396, 408, 414, 416
Buzan, Tony, 84, 399, 412
calm, 177, 181, 218, 227
cancer, 92, 179, 314
carbohydrates, 130
carbon, 24, 64, 130-31, 316, 399
carbon dioxide, 64, 316
carefreeness, 212
catalyst, 303
cause, 14, 19, 49, 134-36
cause-effect, 102, 280, 364

INDEX

celibacy, 180, 405
cell, 121, 133, 403
chance, 78-80
chemistry, 153-54
choice, 72-74, 80, 150, 169
choice maker, 72, 74, 80, 150, 169
classical mechanics, 58, 78-9, 396-97
clear comprehension, 111-12, 143
coarseness of mind, 325-26
cognitive process, 28-29, 148-51
color, 124-25
coma, 29, 146, 170
comfort zone, 311
compassion, 243-46, 283, 342, 353-61
competitiveness, 198
computational agents, 83
computer, 33, 44, 61, 83, 93, 175, 305
conceit, 195-97, 200
concentration, 99, 177-78, 184, 218-19, 220-22, 325-30
concept, 41, 43, 48, 50
conception, 32, 144, 147
conceptual proliferation, 201
concrete matter, 137, 403
conditionality, 71, 85, 102-03, 135, 201, 309
consciousness, 11-30, 49, 85-86, 132-33, 141-43, 151-52, 301, 331-32, 360-62
    all-pervading, 196
    ballet of, 152
    birth, 144
    blissful conscious, 362
    body, 143
    classification of, 146
    death, 144
    definition of, 11-30
    deluded, 142
    determining, 145
    dynamics of, 148
    ear, 15, 31, 143
    eternal, 21
    eye, 19, 143
    father, 21
    functional, 19, 31, 144
    greedy, 142
    hateful, 142
    investigating, 144
    love, 240-41
    mind, 120, 128
    mind-enabling, 144
    mother, 21
    non-deluded, 143
    non-greedy, 143
    non-hateful, 143
    nose, 143, 148
    pure, 54-55, 91, 197, 229
    receiving, 143
    registering, 144
    resultant, 19, 143
    sense-enabling, 31, 144
    source of, 33
    tongue, 31, 143
    types of, 20-21, 141

the ultimate reality, 17
universal, 21
unwholesome, 19-20, 65, 142
wholesome, 19-20, 65, 142
conservation, 273, 397
contact, 157-58, 184, 331-32
contemplation, 162, 174-77, 214, 275, 334-37
contentment, 143, 190, 276-78, 288-89, 324
control, 110, 167, 183, 229, 233, 309, 336
core of nothingness, 257
corruption, 195, 212, 223, 250, 269-71
craving, 46, 68, 110, 160, 164, 166, 181, 187-191, 191, 215, 229, 233, 244, 275, 339
creation, 81, 133-135, 150, 405
cultism, 263
dark energy, 134
Darwin, Charles, 83
death, 55, 71, 81, 139, 144, 147, 179, 201, 252, 363, 396, 404
Deep Blue, 83, 88
delusion, 21, 23, 44, 46-47, 68-69, 72-74, 142, 175, 188, 191-93, 206-208, 255, 352
denial, 230, 405
desire, 56, 74, 75, 181-83, 300, 329
destiny, 78-80
digestion, 132, 309
disability, 228
divine, 25, 231, 237, 239-46, 267, 281, 341, 352, 406
DNA, 133, 154
doshas, 124
doubt, 202-03, 220
ear sensitivity, 31, 132, 148
earth, 34-36, 43, 121-23, 136-37, 308-09, 335, 401
Eastman, George, 93, 400
ecstasy, 176, 190, 322
EEG machine, 93
effectiveness, 228, 304
efficacy, 63, 71, 228
effortlessness, 69, 283, 307
ego, 13-14, 18-19, 40, 46-47, 51, 55, 69, 72, 80, 94, 99, 187-88, 190, 233, 250, 255, 259, 266-67, 283, 303, 311, 333-34
Einstein, Albert, 50, 58, 78, 93, 396-97, 403
elation, 176
electricity, 16
electromagnetic force, 61
electrons, 34, 58, 120-21, 125-26, 139, 396
elements, 9, 13-14, 25, 30, 86, 100, 137
  abstract material, 138
  classification of mental, 24
  concrete material, 138
  divine mental, 231, 241
  material, 20, 24, 33-37, 94, 120-39, 367

mental, 20-29, 86, 141-45, 153-56, 383
noble mental, 247-53
of soul, 13-14, 16, 18, 40
root, 188, 190, 192, 237
special mental, 178, 183
ultimate root, 188, 191, 206, 210, 255
ultimate wholesome root, 237
universal mental, 28, 171
universal unwholesome, 207
unwholesome mental, 187, 207
unwholesome root, 192
wholesome mental, 209-10
wholesome root, 237
wise mental, 255-58
embezzlement, 271
embodiment, 176, 179, 215
emotion, 165-67, 312-13, 317, 352
emotional power, 313
Empedocles, 123, 402
emptiness, 54, 70, 297-98, 319, 328, 330-332
empty space, 137, 330
enchantment, 296, 299
energy, 61-64, 121, 180, 194, 199, 293, 407
enlightened master, 5, 55, 147, 163, 226, 232, 396, 408
enlightenment, 6, 9, 40, 49, 53-56, 178, 192, 195, 227, 248, 259, 363-65, 394, 408
entertainment, 45, 205, 278-79, 293, 295, 323
enthusiasm, 182, 235, 344
entity, 17, 19, 23, 30, 44, 49-50, 70-71, 362
entrainment, 295-96, 408
entropy, 119, 400
envy, 198, 245, 356-57
EQ (see intelligence)
equality complex, 196-97, 406
equanimity, 90, 92-94, 100, 103, 110, 159, 161, 217, 228-33, 235, 242-43, 251, 281, 300, 303, 311, 314, 319-20, 323, 334, 341, 352, 357
eternal, 21, 71, 147, 151, 200
ether, 136
ethical force, 60, 88, 169
ethics, 169
evil, 189, 191, 343, 353
evolution, 61, 68, 81, 83, 87-88, 99, 189, 359
exhalation, 107, 315-18, 328
existence, 13, 17, 42, 46, 55, 71, 125, 146
experiential physics, 58
experiential reality, 123
extravagance, 272
extremism, 200, 222, 225
eye, 15, 31, 143, 148
Eysenck, Hans, 84, 412
faculty, 226
faith, 51-52, 222-23, 283, 406
fanaticism, 200, 225

fasting, 180, 278, 405
fate, 78-80
fear, 66, 107, 155, 180, 312, 354
feeling, 21-23, 28, 87-92, 98,
    158-65, 171, 335-36, 396
  neither pleasant nor
    unpleasant, 159, 161-62
  neutral, 159, 161-62, 234
  physiological, 160-61, 163,
    274, 291
  psychological, 160-61
  pleasant, 289, 291-92, 311, 345
  unpleasant, 28, 92, 159, 163,
    206, 232
fetus, 32
fight-or-flight response, 252
fire, 23, 34, 40, 123, 138, 148,
    401
first cause, 49, 135-36
five sense types, 143, 149
flavors, 31, 289
flexibility, 228, 237, 283, 308
flow, 17, 19, 21, 71, 146-47, 170,
    212, 304
flux, 17, 120, 138
FM modulation, 33
focus, 103, 177, 218
fondness, 242, 244
forbearance, 143, 191
force, 58-68, 70-71, 86, 132,
    147, 169, 397, 399
forgiveness, 99, 284, 347, 352
frames of mind, 113
future, 48, 71

galaxy, 129
Gandhi, Mahatma, 252, 413
Gardner, Howard, 82-84,
    398-99
general intelligence factor, 82
general relativity, 137, 397, 403
generosity, 59, 65, 143, 206, 209,
    212, 270
genetics, 133, 365, 403
gladness, 231-32, 245-46,
    356-57, 359-60
glory, 360
god, 49-51, 99, 129, 135, 200,
    223-25, 283
godly beings, 239
Goleman, Daniel, 83, 398
grace, 223, 237
grand unifying force, 62
gravity, 60, 85, 127-29, 137, 147,
    397, 402
greed, 21-23, 28-29, 65, 67, 100,
    103, 107, 142, 160, 166,
    187-97, 206-08, 266
Greenspan, Stanley, 83, 398
gurus, 101
happiness, 160, 176-77, 211,
    322, 361
Harvard University, 82-84, 398
hatred, 21-23, 28, 40, 47, 64, 67,
    100, 103, 155, 160, 168,
    188, 190-91, 193, 212-13,
    342, 353
healing, 77, 290-93, 299, 408
health, 6, 275, 292, 307

INDEX

heart, 31-34, 56, 132-33, 147, 149, 341, 354, 408
heat, 40, 48, 70, 103, 105, 123, 233, 243, 335
heaven, 51, 223, 341
helium, 131, 171
hell, 341
Himalayas, 124
Hindu, 44, 124, 147
Hippocrates, 124
Hitler, Adolph, 42
holocaust, 42
holy, 191, 242
holy grail, 81
humors, 124
hydrocarbon, 131
hydrogen, 13, 24, 39, 87, 126, 130-32, 134, 171, 399
I-atom, 130-33
ignorance, 14, 17, 35, 40, 47, 189, 191, 193, 255-57
ill will, 189-90, 244, 344
illusion, 13, 17, 48, 71, 94, 136, 176, 255
imbalance, 124, 274, 312
immodesty, 195, 223
immorality, 195, 222
impartiality, 225, 283, 359
impatience, 142, 194
imperfection, 14, 180, 192, 200, 202
impermanence, 48, 90, 103, 138-39, 197, 216-17, 226, 288, 364, 394

impersonality, 138-39, 196, 408
imprisonment, 44, 67-68, 247, 354
impropriety, 195, 223
impulse, 73, 150
inclination, 181-82, 206
indifference, 142, 162, 231-32, 235, 362
Indus valley, 124
inertia, 308-09
inferiority complex, 196
infinity, 330-33
inhalation, 315-17
injustice, 250, 282
intellect, 14, 44, 50-52, 55, 86, 93, 205
intelligence, 14, 19, 82-86, 98-100, 114, 128
  artificial, 87
  definition of, 284
  emotional (EQ), 6, 83, 88, 398
  existential, 84
  general (IQ), 82
  higher levels of, 88, 100, 105, 266, 342
  ladder of, 94, 113, 278
  perfect, 6, 14, 47, 50, 56, 95, 139, 162, 175, 190-91, 196-97, 219-20, 235, 258, 282, 334, 339
  primitive element of, 87
  redefining, 85
  social, 83

soul, 6, 81-82, 84-86, 89-90, 92-94, 98, 100, 104, 112, 299, 342, 397
  spiritual (SQ), 6, 81, 83-85, 91, 342
  types of, 86, 88-91
  what is, 82-86
intelligent
  attitude, 263
  breathing, 315
  eating, 288
  exercising, 307
  hearing, 293
  heart, 341
  seeing, 296
  smelling, 292
  touching, 290
intention, 181-82, 288, 291-94, 304-05, 308, 317, 335
intoxicants, 221, 251, 274-75
introspection, 98
intuition, 84
IQ test, 82-83, 93, 398
jealousy, 198, 245, 356-57, 359
Jesus, 99, 239-40, 347, 355
joy, 12, 48, 78, 143, 162-63, 176, 190, 214, 234, 245, 322, 336, 345, 356
Kalapa, 124
karma, 59-79, 213, 224, 282-84, 346-47, 358
karmic force, 169
karmic retribution, 164

Kasparov, Gary, 83
kindness, 59, 66, 239-40, 341, 357
King, David, 84
knowingness, 156, 170
knowledge, 17-18, 34, 56, 89, 91, 94, 142, 162, 217, 364-65
Laser Interferometer (LIGO), 129
laws of karma, 65-72, 282-84
lethargy, 155, 203, 228
life, 29, 61, 81, 132, 146, 170, 322, 339
life continuum, 146
light, 17, 47, 147, 170, 256, 407
lightness, 138, 227, 283, 312, 319, 327
lipids, 130
living matter, 130-34
Locke, Edwin, 84
logic, 83, 87, 93, 288, 322
love, 59, 88, 94, 240-46, 341-46, 348, 356-57, 359-62
  consciousness, 239-40
  fall in, 357
  four elements of, 342, 359-60
  heart full of, 341
  rise in, 357
  romantic, 242
loving-kindness, 239-45
luck, 78-80
lust, 73, 94, 107, 165, 180-81, 187-88, 271-72, 298, 312-13, 316

INDEX

lying, 195, 212, 247, 251, 268-69
madness, 196
magic, 296, 298
Mahabhutas, 124
male, 132
mango, 18, 65-66
King, Martin Luther, Jr., 252
martyrdom, 200
masked enemies, 242
mass, 34, 119-20, 123, 137, 399, 407
material, 11-12, 15, 31, 361, 404
   base, 31-32, 145
   elements, 20, 33-37, 130-34, 308, 367
   life, 130
   phenomenon, 12, 21, 120, 123, 130
   universe, 282
   voidness, 137
materialism, 84, 120, 139, 226
materiality-mentality, 257
matrix, 44-45
matter, 12-13, 15-17, 24, 30-35, 40, 51, 62, 119-128, 130-38, 146, 160, 169, 331-32, 361-62
   abstract, 136, 138
   attributes of, 138
   concrete, 137
   non-concrete, 137
   inorganic, 15, 153
   living matter, 130-34
   non-organic, 15-16, 31
   organic, 15-16, 31
   origin of, 133, 135
   smallest recognizable unit of, 124, 130
   subtle, 31
   subtle-heart, 132
   types of, 15
   ultimate building blocks of, 33, 119
maturity, 205
maya, 43-47
Mcginn, Colin, 88
meanness, 205, 244-45, 353-56
mechanics, 20, 57-58
meditation, 24, 65, 74, 98, 175, 189, 204-05, 219, 226, 230, 257, 266, 278, 325
   definition of, 98
   for cultivating compassion, 353-55
   for cultivating gladness, 356-57
   for cultivating loving-kindness, 342-52
   for cultivating oneness, 357-59
   for developing breath awareness, 108-12
   for developing austerity, 279
   for developing contentment, 277
   for developing non-indulgence, 273
   for developing non-stealing, 270
   for developing non-violence, 267

for developing physical purity, 275
for developing self-study, 280
for developing sexual piety, 271
for developing surrender, 282
for developing truthfulness, 269
for experiencing infinity and soul, 330, 339
for experiencing zero, 325-330
for intelligent breathing, 315-19
for intelligent eating, 288-90
for intelligent exercising, 307-310
for intelligent hearing, 293-96
for intelligent seeing, 296-99
for intelligent smelling, 292-93
for intelligent touching, 290-92
for intelligent work habits, 304-07
for managing emotions and addictions, 312-315
for pain management, 310-11
for transcending, 321-24
lifestyle of, 104
object of, 107, 110
soul, 97-102, 104
meditativity, 73-74, 77, 104, 108, 194, 198, 205, 266, 309
memory, 18, 82, 89, 147, 168, 215, 311
mental phenomenon, 12, 21, 26-27, 65, 85

absorption, 184
energy, 181
force, 60-61
life, 28-29, 170, 322
power, 177-78, 180-81, 185, 219-21
refinement, 155
rigidity, 200-01
rust, 201
unhealthiness, 228
weaknesses, 220-21
metabolism, 132
microscope, 15, 31, 82, 121, 218
middle way, 78, 229, 394
mid-life crisis, 77, 253
mind, 11-17, 19, 21, 24, 30, 33, 47, 49, 55, 64-66, 86, 99, 113, 120, 136-37, 146, 148, 153-56, 156, 189, 209, 211-13, 218-24, 227, 229, 232, 235, 256-57, 266, 277, 279, 316-17, 319, 321-26, 329-30, 332-39
divine, 25, 239-40, 242-43, 406
noble, 25, 247-51
primordial, 171
special, 173-76, 178, 180-85
sensitivity, 31-33, 132, 148
ultimate building blocks of, 21, 25, 153
universal, 25, 90, 157, 170, 405
unwholesome, 25, 90-91, 187-88, 206

wholesome, 25, 90, 191, 209-10, 215
wise, 25, 255-56
mindfulness, 73, 77, 99-104, 112, 161, 163-64, 170, 177-78, 181, 213-22, 294-95, 297-98, 310, 312, 344, 349, 402
MIT, 84
moderation, 105, 272-73, 323, 394
moods, 110, 214, 230
Moore's Law, 83
moral recklessness, 23, 188, 195, 207-08
morality, 195, 207, 223, 266
motion, 34, 59, 61, 63, 85, 123, 128, 133
motivation, 183
multiple intelligences, 83-84
mythology, 201
narcissism, 196
natural breath, 107, 109-10
negativity, 142, 200, 295
neither perception nor non-perception, 234, 332-33
neither pleasure nor pain, 232, 234
nervous system, 133
Newton, Isaac, 78, 136, 396-97
Newtonian mechanics, 58, 84, 396
nirvana, 6, 55, 395-96
nirvanic peace, 334

nitrogen, 130, 399
Nobel Prize, 93
nobility, 247-48, 250, 252
noble action, 249, 251
Noble, Kathleen, 84
noble ones, 248, 250, 252
noble speech, 247, 251-52
noble vocation, 252-53
non-attachment, 162, 210, 212, 235, 283, 322, 324
non-being, 55
non-belief, 202
non-believer, 50
non-concrete matter, 137
non-delusion, 73, 91, 103, 141, 181, 193, 210-11, 255-59, 266
non-distraction, 194
non-existence, 55, 187, 197, 331-32
non-faith, 202
non-greed, 74, 90, 154, 174, 181, 209-213, 234, 236, 266, 271, 273
non-hatred, 23, 74, 90, 142
non-indulgence, 265, 272-73
non-matter, 331
non-meanness, 244-45, 354
non-perception, 234, 332-33
non-reaction, 73, 99-101, 103, 112, 114, 163-65, 291, 295, 298, 319, 407
non-reality, 40-43, 46-51
    definition of, 41
    test of, 43

non-relative, 283
non-resistance, 283
non-self, 94, 103, 139, 226, 258, 362, 364
non-stealing, 265, 270-71
non-striving, 69
non-violence, 267-68
nose sensitivity, 31, 132, 148
nostrils, 108-09, 216, 317, 325-26, 330
nothingness, 257, 331-32, 362
not-ness, 331
nourishment, 73, 288-89
nuclear fusion, 131
nuclear power, 259
nucleic acids, 130
nucleogenesis, 131, 399
nucleosynthesis, 131, 399
nutriment, 125, 132-35
OM, 98, 129, 407
oneness, 54, 84, 143, 271-72, 324, 341-42, 357, 361
out-breath, 111, 317, 327, 335
out-of-body experience (OBE), 408
oxygen, 13, 24, 39, 126, 130-31, 399
pain, 14, 109, 138-39, 158-63, 180, 229-30, 278, 303, 344-45, 354
pain control, 229, 311
pain management, 233, 310
pain-pleasure management, 229
pain-transcendent, 303, 310

parinirvana, 55, 396
particle accelerators, 123, 134
past, 48, 71, 89, 102, 150
patience, 143, 191
Payne, Wayne, 83, 398
peace, 5, 51, 65, 143, 230, 234, 245, 259, 267, 293, 296, 299, 334, 344-45, 354-55
Penrose, Roger, 88, 404
perception, 14, 18, 22, 28, 167-68, 171, 235, 257, 331-34, 396
perfect accounting system, 66, 80
perfect intelligence (see intelligence)
perfect life, 342
perfection, 6, 14, 39, 56, 69-70, 74, 91, 177-78, 189, 197, 219-20, 227, 256, 258, 266, 269, 303, 406
periodic table, 24, 39, 87, 120, 131, 153, 171
personal affection, 242
personal power, 194
perversion, 201
pessimism, 93, 200
phenomenality, 201
phenomenon, 12, 14, 19, 30
philosophy, 120, 124, 395, 402-03, 412
physics, 58, 62, 78, 88, 129, 134, 153, 364

INDEX

pity, 298, 361
planets, 58, 61, 396
Plato, 124, 402-03, 412
pleasant looks, 213
pleasantness, 103, 109, 143, 161-63, 245, 287
pleasure control, 229
pliability, 138, 228
portal of healing, 290
potentiality, 62, 64, 146
poverty, 211-12, 230, 271
prayer, 99, 101, 130, 354
presence of mind, 17, 102, 213
present-moment awareness, 177, 218
peer pressure, 45
pride, 42, 65, 195-96, 207-08, 229, 308
probability, 64, 78-79, 83
process of cognition, 21, 23, 28-29, 150
production, 138
proteins, 130
providence, 78
psychometrics, 82, 398
pure awareness, 6, 50, 90, 112, 217, 259, 338
pure learning, 263
pure understanding, 54-55, 77, 85, 143, 258
purification, 99, 201, 263
purpose of life, 75, 78
quantum mechanics, 9, 57-58, 78-79, 85, 125, 128, 396

quarks, 120, 126, 139, 400
radio waves, 31-33
rapture, 162, 176-77, 184, 220, 318-19, 322, 326
reality, 13, 17, 39-46, 49, 85, 127, 191, 395
   conditional, 40, 146
   definition of, 39-40
   test of, 42-43
   ultimate, 17-18, 23, 34, 40, 47, 50, 120, 122, 156, 200
   unconditional, 53-55
realization, 11, 46, 62, 77, 362
receiver, 31-33
recognition, 250
rectitude, 229, 237
refinement, 165, 221, 311
refinement of pain, 163
reflection, 98, 329, 358
refreshment, 176
regrets, 221
reincarnation, 81
relaxation, 97-98
religious rites, 200
relinquishment, 324, 337-38
remorse, 198-99, 221, 344
renunciation, 143, 183, 230, 235, 324, 329
resentment, 190, 229-30, 241-42, 343-44
resolution, 178-79, 184, 211, 213, 311, 313
restlessness, 188, 193-94, 207, 218, 220-21

Restless-O-Meter, 194
revenge, 178, 354
reverence, 65, 223
right doing, 66, 198
right-force, 183
Rishis, 248
rituals, 76, 200-01, 224, 288
RNA, 130, 154
robots, 83, 88
Rutgers University, 88
sacredness, 292
sadness, 12, 110, 243
safe haven, 107, 222
safety, 344-45, 349
saint, 191
sainthood, 143
saliva, 148
sanctity, 292, 299
sand, 101-02
Searle, John, 88, 399, 404
self, 4, 14, 40, 47-48, 55-56, 68-69, 71, 84-85, 89-90, 94, 103, 142, 167, 171, 176, 180, 191, 195-97, 199-203, 241, 256-58, 276, 338, 352
self-annihilation, 68
self-centered, 74, 212, 241
self-centeredness, 196
self-control, 183, 229
self-defense, 250, 252
self-esteem, 212, 221, 344
self-glorification, 196
self-identity, 78
self-importance, 196

self-improvement, 77, 204, 280
self-interest, 75, 182, 208, 210, 323
selfishness, 68, 142-43
selfless, 68-69, 91
self-mastery, 101
self-mortification, 251
self-realization, 77
self-respect, 195, 207, 222, 271
self-retreat, 325
self-sacrifice, 68, 213
self-study, 3, 265-66, 280-81
semantics, 88
sensitivity, 15, 31-33, 132-33, 148-49, 165, 298
sensual greed, 187
sensual matter, 132
sensuality, 183, 323, 331-32
sex, 187, 275, 300, 323
sexual matter, 132
sexual piety, 265, 271-72
sexual relationship, 271
shame, 169, 222-23, 228, 237, 271
shamelessness, 23, 188, 195, 207-08, 269-71
silence, 54, 77, 129, 204-05, 279, 293-94, 335-36, 408
simplicity, 273
sine frequencies, 33
sixth sense, 133
skepticism, 142, 175, 202
skillfulness, 228, 237
sloth, 155, 174, 193, 203-05, 220, 227, 272, 316

INDEX

slum, 230
smallest recognizable unit of matter, 121-25
smell, 31, 121, 125, 132, 148, 230, 292-93, 299
smile, 4, 111, 306, 349, 360
smoking, 179, 274-75, 312, 314-15
sociability, 143, 236, 295
social service, 182
Socrates, 124
soil, 34, 66, 123, 290, 401
Soul
   beyond, 9, 40, 53, 56, 396
   cognitive process of, 148
   elements of (see elements)
   first element of, 14
   genesis, 132
   individual, 59, 90
   intelligence (see intelligence)
   introduction, 7
   mechanics, 58, 60, 63-80, 88, 125, 127
   meditation (see meditation)
   model, 86
   realization, 6, 263
second element of, 21
   third element of, 30
   what is, 11, 394
   what is not, 39, 395
soul mechanics, 58-79, 104, 125, 127-28, 282, 395, 404
   first law of, 65
   fourth law of, 70
   new scientific frontier, 58
   second law of, 66-67
   third law of, 68
Soul-atom, 124-30
sound element, 129-30
space, 49, 54, 69, 134, 136-37, 148, 200, 232, 235, 295-97, 305, 319, 330-31, 357, 361, 364, 403
space element, 137
spaceness, 330-31
space-time, 59, 61, 85, 136
spectrum, 112, 233
spirit, 84, 151, 183, 283, 407
spiritual, 19, 24, 33, 49-50, 52, 59, 94, 161, 175, 180, 195
   equanimity, 233-34
   evolution, 189-90, 192, 280, 347
   feet, 181, 217
   hands, 226
   image, 197
   intelligence (see intelligence)
   joy, 12, 111, 162-63, 176
   matter, 120
sentiment, 263
   treasure, 227
   vehicle, 99
   vision, 30, 91-92
SQ (see Intelligence)
Standard Model, 125, 127, 402
stillness, 193, 237, 297-99
sting, 312-14

stinginess, 206
strength of character, 183
stress, 14, 45, 227, 237, 291-92, 323
String Theory, 126-27, 129, 400, 402
stupidity, 65, 353
subatomic particles, 61, 120-21, 125-26, 134
subconscious, 144, 146-50, 170
subtle-heart matter (see matter)
suffering, 14, 44, 46, 73, 100, 138, 142, 167, 170, 189, 192, 194, 243-45, 300, 339, 343-45, 353-55, 359, 364
superiority complex, 196
supersensitive, 232, 288-89, 299
superstition, 175, 189, 193, 199, 220, 225-26, 228, 334
suppression, 110, 313-14
surrender, 223, 265-66, 282-83, 324, 346
suspicion, 202-03, 220, 225-26, 344
syntax, 88
tai chi, 307
taste, 31, 121, 125, 132, 148, 232, 289, 300-01
telescope, 82, 218
temperature, 40, 128, 132-36
temptation, 179
Theory of Everything (TOE), 58, 127, 397

thinking, 15, 18, 21, 82, 88, 90, 99, 145, 170, 173-177, 183-84, 202, 318-19, 322, 325, 334
third eye, 82, 91
Thorndike, Edward, 83, 398
thoughtfulness, 174-77, 184, 203, 220, 319, 322, 326, 334
time, 48-49, 55, 71, 405
timelessness, 70
TOE (see Theory of Everything)
tongue sensitivity, 31, 132, 148
torpor, 155, 174, 193, 203-05, 220, 268, 309, 316
toxins, 275, 316
tranquility, 65, 106, 194, 199, 220-21, 227, 237, 242, 406
tranquilizer, 227
transcendence, 84, 165, 322, 324-25, 333
transience, 287
transmitter, 33
trans-sensual greed, 187
truthfulness, 268-69
Turing, Alan, 93, 404
ultimate, 14, 17-18, 23, 40, 47, 55, 91, 94
   beginning, 48-49
   being, 50
   building blocks, 6, 21, 25-27, 33-34, 36
   end, 48-49
uncertainty, 193, 202, 397

unconditional abstinence, 247-49
undercurrent of silence, 295
understanding, 91-92, 100, 167, 177, 258
universality, 43
universe, 58, 61-62, 78, 80, 122, 129, 134-36, 282, 295, 365, 399, 402
University of California at Berkley, 88
University of Oxford, 88
unmanifest, 64
unpleasantness, 102, 109, 159-66, 191, 310, 336
uranium, 119, 407
vacuum, 134
vanity, 65, 182, 195-96, 208, 308
vibrating string, 126-27, 129
vigor, 179-81, 184, 193, 204-05, 211, 220, 313
vision, 19, 30, 82, 91-92, 111-12, 217, 297, 364
vital energy, 179
vocal intimation, 138
voidness, 137, 331
volition, 15-16, 28-29, 59-70, 72-74, 148, 168, 266
volitional action, 59-62, 64, 70, 73, 150, 169
volitional energy, 61-64, 86, 133-36

volitional force, 60-66, 70-71, 73, 79, 86, 127-28, 130, 132, 147, 149-50, 169-170, 344
volitional formation, 64
volitional universe, 62
wakefulness, 111-12, 204, 217, 279, 339
water, 12-13, 17, 19, 23, 34-35, 41, 59, 62-63, 122-23, 126-27, 130-$\approx$31, 148, 176, 209, 241, 275, 288, 305, 308, 333, 401-02
weightlessness, 328
whole-body awareness, 304, 306-08
will power, 168, 248, 313
wisdom, 47, 85, 91-92, 139, 143, 152, 162, 193, 214, 255-56, 351-52, 358, 364
wise attention, 73, 99-101, 103, 110-13, 193, 217, 232
wonder, 296, 298
worry, 198-99, 212, 220, 227, 269, 283, 344
wrongdoing, 66, 77, 198, 247-49, 251
yoga, 5, 307, 394, 405, 407
yogi, 99, 128
zero, 126, 136, 325, 328, 330
Zohar, Danah, 84, 399
zygote, 133

About the Author

Sam Adettiwar is a master's graduate of engineering from Auburn University, a successful entrepreneur, a practitioner of yoga and martial arts, a devout meditator, and a spiritual scientist. As the founder and director of Soul Research Institute, he is engaged in spiritual research, writing, and teaching. He currently lives in the foothills of the Rocky Mountains in Colorado with his wife and two children. For information on his awakening experience, research themes, cutting edge meditation techniques, and retreats, please visit soulresearchinstitute.org.

www.ingramcontent.com/pod-product-compliance
Lightning Source LLC
Chambersburg PA
CBHW022045160426
43198CB00008B/134